LETTERS FROM THE SAINTS

*Early Renaissance and Reformation Periods
from St. Thomas Aquinas to Bl. Robert Southwell*

LETTERS FROM THE SAINTS

✠ ✠ ✠

*Early Renaissance and Reformation Periods
from St. Thomas Aquinas to Bl. Robert Southwell*

COMPILED BY
CLAUDE *Charles H.* WILLIAMSON

*Omnes Sancti et Sanctae Dei,
intercedite pro nobis*

SALISBURY SQUARE · LONDON

BY REV. CLAUDE WILLIAMSON

To the memory of my father, and in
deep affection to my mother

MADE AND PRINTED IN GREAT BRITAIN BY
WYMAN AND SONS LIMITED, LONDON, FAKENHAM AND READING

PREFACE

IT was while sailing among the many beautiful islands of the South
Pacific that I mused concerning the loneliness of those Europeans
who were forced to live there, or who did so voluntarily, as in the
case of missionaries. Away from western noise and turmoil, life
would be generally placid and a letter from home most welcome.
From such thoughts my mind wandered on to the giving and receiving of letters, and I thought of the accounts written over the past
2,000 years by missionaries; and others to those at home. I then
decided to make a collection of letters written by hermits and saints,
and the following letters I copied from various books in libraries
as far away as Hong Kong, New Zealand, America and South Africa.

No documents are of greater importance for the proper understanding of the history of any period than the correspondence of men
and women of affairs; and though many of the letters in this volume
were written by recluses, yet they have had in many cases almost as
much effect as those written by officials and teachers of the Church.

The letters I have collected here have not been chosen with any
pre-conceived view of instruction or the elucidation of obscure
points. Writers with a bulky output afford a much more difficult
choice when it comes to selecting extracts for illustration. On the
other hand in many cases only one letter, or even part of a letter, has
survived the centuries. The documents date from crucial periods in
the development of Christian culture: their importance for the
history of civilization far transcends that of mere biographical
accuracy, which some of them in fact conspicuously fail to attain.
Their primary value lies in the light they throw on the ideas existent
in their author's mind, thus contributing to inform the mind of
Christendom then and thereafter. The volume may be compared to
a kind of pageant, every scene of which, as it is unrolled before
him, brings the spectator into new company, calls up fresh ideas, and
makes new demands on the knowledge which should be a necessary

v

part of the education of every citizen. Covering such a long period of time, I presume there may be a few errors of fact. In some cases it has not been possible to give the name of the person to whom the letter was addressed. Knowledge of this would be a great help in the understanding of the allusions and other obscure points. But as this is a book for edification and not of erudition, I have not troubled to give exact references as to where the originals are to be found, because this would add scores of pages devoted to technical bibliography. Some authorities give dates which vary by a year or two: no doubt this is due to the variance of reckoning in early medieval times. In the lives of the saints we see the inner life of the Church itself, and how in every age the Christian tradition finds expression in some new creative achievement which is characteristic of its time and place. In the past the lives and legends of the saints played a leading part in Christian teaching and education.

What is the secret and so potent attraction of the saints? The interest in sanctity evidently survives theological and ethical preoccupations. Indeed, today, the saint is perhaps an object of higher intrinsic interest to 'unbelievers' than to the faithful. The saint is one who knows that every moment of our human life is a moment of crisis; for at every moment we are called upon to make an all-important decision—to choose between the ways that lead to death and spiritual darkness, and the way that leads towards light and life; between events exclusively temporal, and the eternal order; between our personal will, or the will of some projection of our personality, and the will of God. In order to fit himself to deal with the emergencies of the way of life, the saint undertakes appropriate training of mind and body, just as a soldier does. For whereas the obligations of military training are limited and generally very simple, namely to make men courageous, cool-headed and co-operatively efficient in the cause of killing men with whom they have no personal quarrel—the objects of spiritual training are much less narrowly specialized. Here the aim is primarily to bring human nature to a state in which there are no 'God-eclipsing' obstacles between themselves and God, and to meet the obstacles always without malice, greed and self-assertion. It follows that spiritual training is more difficult than military training. Nevertheless, the important position of the saint in the Catholic economy does tend to conceal his real personality from his worshippers. He inevitably tends to be considered more as a means to an end, than as an object intrinsically worthy of contemplation. The saints lived sparsely and chastely, and the mortifications of the twin appetites of hunger and love represent to the ordinary man the acme of self-control. The biography of a saint (who is always ascetic) is valuable only in so far as it throws light upon the means by which, in the circumstances of a particular human life, the ego is purged away so as to make room for the divine 'not I'. The positive quality of a saint is love expressing itself through joy. External conditions varied, often grotesque, almost always terrible. Their inmost spirit was their most-cherished possession. Saints are never half-hearted, but single-hearted and, however great their intellectual gifts, preferably simple.

To use Shelley's familiar phrase, true letter-writing is 'unpremeditated art'. As will be seen from the following selection of letters written by saints, the earlier writers generally devote their matter to important statements of dogma and historical facts, whereas the later ones dwell mostly upon individuals. And we should all be the poorer if we did not inherit and sometimes re-read the letters purposely written to make clear a matter and to advise or cheer as the case may be. We can be thoroughly sure that none were composed with an eye on posterity but only for immediate edification. Of course it may be true that some have lost the personal touch by translation. The emphasis in the typical Latin saint's life is upon *mirabilia* rather than *memorabilia*. But as the vernacular lives increased in popularity they decreased in value as biographies. Regarded as a type of literary biography, these books had the merits of the exclusion of irrelevant material, of concentrated unity in a central figure, and of a definite purpose. Great men do not always write great letters. Regarding the letters in this collection, many were written in the 'worst' periods; but even if period or author be 'good', the letters are not necessarily the best work of either, judged by a severely classic standard. A few are even illiterate: the illiterate ones are perhaps the most precious, far lovelier than the more gaudy literary flowers of some of the more illustrious pens.

Even a hasty reading of these letters (which are arranged in chronological order) will disclose the fact that nearly all the early ones are concerned with the momentous affairs of a world of alarms and horrors; and as the world grows older the emphasis shifts to the private doings of individuals in the unsteadiness of civilization and the loss of spiritual hope. It is surely no accident that we know Christ's apostles mainly through their letters, or that their ministry was addressed to the absent almost as much as to the present.

Like ourselves, some of the saints detested writing letters and others enjoyed it thoroughly. St. Leonard of Port Maurice corresponded with kings and others of high rank; but a complaint was made against him that he wrote most of them on old, odd scraps of paper. In the Ages of Faith, letter-writing was cultivated as a real art and by none more so than those in the cloisters trying hard to become saints and inheritors of the Kingdom of God.

We cannot be far wrong in saying that the saint of today will be distinguished by a remarkable perfection of his human characteristics. Indeed, it may be no exaggeration to say that this age will never believe in any saint unless it can believe in him first as being in the fullest sense a man. Whether one reads the letters of St. Paul or those of St. François de Sales, the gist of the matter is the meeting between the natural and the supernatural. We cannot imagine a saint except as one who was in the natural sense perfect, noble and pure of heart, truthful and childlike, devoted, whatever his endowments might be, to beauty, goodness and truth. Supernatural virtue does not curtail natural virtue.

Finally I have to thank Messrs. Burns & Oates Ltd., J. M. Dent Ltd., A. & C. Black Ltd., Sheed & Ward, George Bell Ltd., and Virtue & Co. Ltd., for generous permission to quote from books of which they hold the copyright. Also the Rev. Peter Jamieson, M.A., for help in translation, and Mr. David Watmough for many suggestions and general improvement to an untidy manuscript and for gracious help in assembly.

CLAUDE WILLIAMSON

CONTENTS

A*   ix

St. Thomas Aquinas

c. 1225–1274

Brother John, most dear to me in Christ: Since you have asked me how one should set about to acquire the treasure of knowledge, this is my advice to you concerning it: namely, that you should choose to enter, not straightway into the ocean, but by way of the little streams; for difficult things ought to be reached by way of easy ones.

The following, therefore, is my advice to you concerning your way of living:

I urge you to hesitate before speaking, and to hesitate before visiting the common room;

Hold fast to the cleanness of your conscience;

Do not cease from devoting time to prayer;

Love your cell by making constant use of it, if you want to be admitted into the wine-cellar;

Show yourself to be lovable to everybody, or at least try to do so; but be very familiar with nobody, for too much familiarity breeds contempt and introduces factors which retard study;

Also, do not in any way get yourself involved in the doings and sayings of outsiders;

Avoid aimless meandering above all things;

Do not fail to follow in the footsteps of the saints and of sound men;

Do not heed *by whom* a thing is said, but rather *what* is said you should commit to your memory;

What you read, set about to understand, verifying what is doubtful;

Strive to put whatsoever you can in the cupboard of your mind, as though you were wanting to fill a vessel to the brim;

'Seek not the things that are too high for thee';

Follow in the footsteps of that blessed Dominic, who, while he yet had life for his fellow-traveller, brought forth and produced foliage, blossom, fruit—fruit both serviceable and astonishing—in the vineyard of the Lord of Hosts. If you shall have followed these steps, you will be able to attain to whatsoever you have a mind. Fare you well!

THOMAS AQUINAS was born near the little town of Aquino in Italy. He received his early education at Monte Cassino, in the great Benedictine monastery, which was quite near his home. When ten years old he was sent to the University of Naples, and before he was seventeen he had received the white habit of St. Dominic in spite of active opposition from his family. He was shortly afterwards sent by the Superior-General of his Order to Cologne, to receive instruction from Albertus Magnus, a Dominican Professor, one of the greatest thinkers of his period. St. Thomas, now free for the first time, gave his whole life to prayer and study. His great stature, and his silent and absorbed demeanour, led to his being nick-named 'The Dumb Ox'. When Albertus Magnus was sent to Paris in 1245, St. Thomas accompanied him, and afterwards returned with him to Cologne.

Aquinas had an especial devotion to the Blessed Sacrament. He obtained from the Pope the annual observance of Corpus Christi Day, for which he composed the office. Two of his great works are the *Catena Aurea*, or *Golden Chain*, and his *Summa of Theology*, which occupied the last nine years of his life. He wrote this famous work in the intervals of long and tedious journeys, daily preachings, lectures, and disputations. His death came before he had quite finished it. In spite of his magnificent intellectual powers he is said to have had the simplicity of a child. When asked what was the greatest favour God had granted him, he replied, 'I think it is that of having understood whatever I read.' Just before his death he seems to have received a wonderful revelation, and seen and heard unspeakable things, in comparison with which, he said, all that he had written appeared to him as so much straw. After this he wrote no more. He was only fifty when he died. He was canonized in 1323, and in 1567 the title of Doctor of the Church was conferred upon him.

The above letter, to the best of my knowledge, is the only one extant of St. Thomas. It is addressed to a 'Brother John'—presumably a fellow-member of the Order of Preachers.

Bl. Angela of Foligno

Mmy little children, what I say unto you, I say not, save only for the love of God, and because I promised you that I would not of my own will carry aught away with me under the earth that might be profitable unto you. For it hath pleased God in His goodness to give me the care and solicitude of His daughters, and I have kept them as well as I was able. And now, O my God, I give them back to Thee, and I ask of Thee, by Thine own unutterable love, to guard them from every evil, and to keep them in every good, in the love of poverty, contempt and sorrow, and the transformation and imitation of Thy life and perfection, which Thou hast been pleased to show unto us by word and deed and in Thy living life.

Oh! my most loving little children, I exhort you in this my last exhortation, to strive to be little, and truly humble and meek, not only outwardly in your works, but much more in the depths of your heart, that ye may be true scholars and true disciples of Him Who said: 'Learn of Me, for I am meek and lowly of heart.' O unknown nothing! Of a truth the soul can have no better vision nor knowledge than to see her own nothingness, and to stand in her own prison.

O my little children, strive to have charity, without which there is neither salvation nor merit, and I exhort you, not only to desire to have this charity one for another, but also for all mankind. Judge no man; and if ye shall

4

see a man sin mortally, I say not that the sin should not be displeasing unto you, and that you ought not to abhor the sin; but I say that ye should not judge the sinner nor despise him, for ye know not the judgements of God. And many are there who before men seem to be saved, who before God are already reprobate.

I make no other testament, save that I recommend unto you mutual love and profound humility. And I leave unto you all my inheritance, which is also that of Christ Jesus, that is poverty, sorrow and contempt, namely, the life of Christ. They who shall have this inheritance of the life of Christ shall be my children; for they are the sons of God, and there is no doubt but that afterwards they will inherit life everlasting.

ANGELA'S birthplace was Foligno, near Assisi, where she was born about the year 1249. As a child she received some religious teaching, but her education was neglected, for they did not think much of such things in the days when Angela lived. She married a rich noble when quite young. But she never achieved happiness, for she was self-indulgent and spent her life in pleasure. Often there would come to her mind the thought of what her mother had taught her when she was a little child, and of the good St. Francis and his holy life of poverty and good works, for he lived quite close to their own home, at Assisi.

It is said that when Angela wilfully sinned against her husband or children, or broke one of God's commandments, she well knew that if death were to overtake her in that condition her soul would be lost, and yet knowing this she found it hard to summon up courage enough to break with her bad habits.

But God, as he often does, led the soul of Angela back to Himself by a great affliction and sorrow which He sent her, for she lost in death almost at one time her husband, children, and mother. She was greatly affected by the sudden way in which death had come and removed those closest to her, and was full of alarm lest she herself should be taken away before she had time to repent. Angela therefore determined to give up her bad habits and companions; and to help her repentance she joined the Third Order of St. Francis. But Angela, after much self-indulgence, found it very hard truly to repent and amend. She was, we are told, afraid to make a full confession of her sins, partly because she feared the penance that might be given her, and partly because she was ashamed of the sins into which she had fallen. In this state it is no wonder that the devil is said to have tempted her again. When she came to look back on the conflict that she endured in those days, she said that she would rather suffer the tortures of martyrdom or the pains of any disease than face once more the fierce temptations and assaults of Satan. After two years of great conflict God gave her real peace and her heart was full of love for Him, Whom she now began to love above all things.

In a book which Angela wrote, which she called *Visions and Instructions* (the original copy of which is now in the British Museum), she tells the story of her repentance, saying that while she was trying to repent she passed through as many as eighteen stages before she came to see and realize the sinfulness of her life. She died in the year 1309.

The above letter of Bl. Angela was dictated to unknown recipients, though possibly to a group of nuns.

Bl. John Ruysbroeck

1293–1381

My DEAREST SISTER,

Reflect how Christ, the Son of God, humbled and emptied Himself, taking the form of a servant to serve us. He was meek, merciful and obedient to His heavenly Father unto death and all for our sake. Amid His disciples He willed to appear as a servant declaring that He had come not to be ministered to but to minister (Matt. xx, 28). Wherefore He has been exalted in His humanity and God has given Him a name above all names so that, as St. Paul says, 'In the name of Jesus every knee shall bow in heaven, on earth and in hell.'

If, therefore, the Eternal Wisdom of God has deliberately chosen to minister to the poor, to slaves and to sinners, with what good will should you serve and give your obedience to God and your superiors! Nor should you set a high price on your service either, but reckon as far more valuable the fact that God deigns to accept it. Were you indeed the Empress of Rome and mistress of the whole world and were you to leave it all to become a poor servant to minister to Christ in His members, you might thereby rejoice with a great joy, because in all truth a great blessing and high honour had been bestowed on you.

The most splendid glory and the loftiest dignity that can in fact be attained in the whole world, if we reckon things at their true worth, is the service of God. To serve God wisely means to possess and reign in an everlasting kingdom, and although this kingdom be at present hidden within us, it will be revealed hereafter when Christ shall say: 'Good and faithful servant, enter thou into the joy of thy Lord.' Thus, all whose wish it is to be masters and mistresses, to serve none but to be served, have no place in the kingdom of God. That is why the Pope of Rome calls himself the servant of the servants of God, and as such he ought to consider himself in the spiritual ministrations and for the advantage of holy Christendom if he wishes to follow Christ and reign with Him.

But I must teach my sister how to accomplish her service with humility and purity, as a daughter of God and one worthy of receiving the crown of virginity and the hundredfold reward. Hear then what the prophet David says: 'Hearken, O daughter, and see and incline thy ear, and forget thy people and thy father's house. And the King shall greatly desire thy beauty.' It is for this reason, my dear sister, that I beg you to hearken to God and your superior, to see and consider all that they command, and to incline your ear to every obedience, for then shall the King, who is Christ, desire your beauty.

In the morning, after hearing Mass, go straight to your work. If your task is such that you can neither hear Mass nor receive Holy Communion do not be upset about it; God loves obedience better than sacrifices, and the merit of renouncing one's own will is invariably greater and more precious than getting one's own way. For this reason you should always choose the humblest, most despised duties, whether it be in the kitchen or in the infirmary. Never speak peremptorily and do not give orders to anyone unless you have been told to do so, but cheerfully do yourself whatever lies within your power. If the work commanded you be of the most menial kind, rejoice and give God thanks for considering you worthy of it. If you are given charge of the sick and weak, serve them with

8

joy, sweetness and humility and without any grumbling. If they prove difficult and irritable, consider how you are serving Christ and let your countenance show forth such sweetness and affection that they may stand ashamed before God and man. Do not stop short at the patient but look beyond to God for Whose sake you are nursing her. Take the greatest care not to depress the sick or to upset them by the way you speak or act or by the attitude you adopt towards them; if you see that they are sad and fretful, console them by recalling to them the sufferings of our Lord and the saints, the joy with which they bore them, and the glory and bliss of everlasting life which they consequently enjoy. When the sick really need anything, make all possible haste to procure it for them. When, on the other hand, they ask for something that would be neither good for them nor useful but might rather increase their ailments, pretend that you have not heard or have not understood. If they insist on having it, tell them simply that it would do them harm. If they refuse to give in, go and ask advice from your superior or from those of riper experience than yourself.

Let everything that you prepare for the sick in the way of food and drink be done properly and make it look as dainty as possible so that it will give them pleasure and peace will reign on both sides. Make their beds yourself and keep up their spirits as far as you can, in proportion as they are very weak or need comforting. Stay close to them and watch over them if necessary. Radiate joy and cheerfulness, and chat with them so light-heartedly that the sick will all have a welcome for you. Approach serious topics as well if they will let you, and place before them the example of our Lord and the saints, so that all who come in contact with you may receive also spiritual food for their souls.

When sickness comes your own way, look upon yourself as a poor pilgrim lodged in a stranger's house, homesick for his eternal fatherland. Be patient, cheerful and resigned in all things, giving thanks to God for His gifts. Show no preferences, no longing for anything save what God pleases to give you. You must not let yourself concentrate too much and worry over the state of your own health, but rest content with everything, abandoning yourself completely to God, and do not utter any complaint either of your sickness or weariness or of the fickleness of others. Even when nobody has come to see you, neither grumble about it nor pass any judgement, but accept from the hand of God all that it is His will to lay upon you.

If you can, eat and drink all that is given you as if you were a beggar. If it chance to be too salt, or burnt, or disagreeable, consider how, in the midst of most terrible sufferings, Our Lord was given gall and vinegar as meat and drink, yet He held His peace and made no complaint. Do you, in like manner, bear all for His sake. Check your wants and do not ask for everything that you happen to feel you would like, because that is how the rich and fastidious are wont to behave, but it ill becomes the poor and is likely to cause displeasure and pain to onlookers. If you are forgotten and no one comes near you when you stand in real need of someone, lie there patiently and quite unruffled in spite of it all, because it is at such times that Christ draws nigh with the angels and saints. And when you are up and better, go back humbly to the task appointed you without making any choice of your own; go where you are sent, be it the scullery, the infirmary or the kitchen. Be simple, prudent and faithful in the discharge of your duty. Be always gracious, cheerful and obliging towards those with whom you live, avoiding all singularity and ready to do what anyone and everyone asks of you.

If when you are called to the parlour or told to go, you find yourself light-hearted at the prospect and nothing loth, you should feel uneasy because it proves that you are living according to the flesh and not according to the spirit, and you are not yet versed in the simple rudiments of enclosure and all that it really means. When you go to the grille, let not your habit be over-scrupulously neat, nor let it be slovenly, but keep a happy mean. Upon presenting yourself, keep your eyes cast down and avoid fixing anyone with a direct stare. Salute your visitors simply, in a few words. If they happen to be religious, ask them to tell you something edifying and profitable to your soul, to teach you to remain faithful to your vows and the cloister till the end of your life. If, however, they are worldly-minded, be very careful of your words for fear they find matter for criticism and scandalous gossip, and keep your distance from the grate, yet near enough to allow of your visitors' hearing all you say and vice versa. Do not ask anyone for a gift or suggest a suitable one; likewise neither give nor receive a gift without your superior's leave. Finally, as soon as ever you can, leave behind you the troubles of people of the world and all conversation and association with them, and return to your solitude with God. If you find pleasure in going to the parlour and prefer to dissipate yourself in outward things rather than concentrate your energies on an interior life, if you love discussing and hearing tittle-tattle and worldly news, it will be impossible to receive interior light, and darkness and heaviness will engulf you increasingly day by day. Embrace your contemplative life with all your heart therefore, and keep a strict enclosure.

JOHN RUYSBROECK was born near Brussels in 1293 and is one of the most famous of mystical writers. After his ordination he lived with his uncle, a secular canon, and then at the age of fifty withdrew with others to Groenendaal in the forest of Soignies and formed a community of contemplative Augustinian canons regular. Bl. John was an exemplary religious and he exercised a great influence on his contemporaries; among his writings are the *Adornment of the Spiritual Marriage* and the *Book of the Spiritual Tabernacle*. He died in 1381.

Without following Maeterlinck in his extravagant eulogy of Ruysbroeck, it must be admitted that his great *Ordo spiritualium nuptialium*, is one of the most valuable works of its kind that exists, marking as it does with intense force and lofty teaching the mystic ascent, and describing with extreme precision and astonishing fulness the steps on the way. He seems to have read Dionysius, St. Augustine, Eckhart, and other suitable writers; but the unsurpassed depth of his thought and spiritual acumen is without doubt due to first-hand spiritual experience.

The above letter is addressed to a nun.

Bl. Henry Suso

1295-1365

MY DEAR DAUGHTER,
 If your purpose is to order your spiritual
life according to my teaching, as was your request to me,
cease from all such austerities, for they suit not the weakness of your sex and your well-ordered frame. The dear
Jesus did not say: 'Take My cross upon you'; but He said
to each: 'Take up thy cross.' You should not seek to
imitate the austerities of the ancient fathers, nor the severe
exercises of your spiritual father. You should only take
for yourself a portion of them, such as you can easily practise with an infirm body to the end that sin may die in you
and yet your bodily life may not be shortened.

 It is written that, in former times, some among the
ancient fathers led a life of such superhuman and incredible
austerity, that the very mention of it is a horror to certain
delicate persons of the present day; for they know not
what burning devotion can enable a man, by the divine
aid, to do and suffer for God. One who is filled with such
fervour finds all impossible things become possible of
accomplishment in God; just as David says, that with God's
help we will go through a wall (Ps. xvii, 30). It is also
written in the book of the ancient fathers that some of them
would not treat themselves with such great severity as
others did, and yet they were all striving to reach the self-
same end. St. Peter and St. John had not the same training.
Who can fully explain this marvel, unless it be that the
Lord Who is wonderful in His saints wills, by reason of

His high sovereignty, to be glorified in many different ways? Besides this, our natures are not all alike, and what is suitable to one suits not another. Therefore it must not be thought, that if perchance a man has not practised such great austerities, he will be thereby hindered from arriving at perfection. At the same time, those who are soft and delicate should not despise austerities in others or judge them harshly. Let each look to himself and see what God wants of him, and attend to this leaving all else alone. Speaking generally, it is much better to be moderate rather than immoderate in the practice of austerities. But as the mean is hard to find it is wiser to keep a little under it than to venture too high above it: for it often happens that if a man mortifies his bodily frame to excess, he will have afterwards to indulge it to excess; though certainly many great saints have forgotten themselves in this point through the fervour of their devotion. Such austerity of life and the examples which have been mentioned may be of use to those who are too tender with themselves, and to their own injury give too much rein to their rebellious bodies: but this concerns not you nor the like of you. God has many kinds of crosses with which He chastens His friends. I look for Him to lay another sort of cross upon your shoulders which will be far more painful to you than these austerities. Accept this cross with patience when it comes to you!

HENRY SUSO was a native of Bihlmeyer, near Constance, who joined the Friars Preachers at an early age, was prior in several houses of the Order, and excelled as a director of souls. He is one of the greatest Dominican mystics and his *Book of the Eternal Wisdom* is still one of the most widely read classics on Christian mysticism. During a great part of his life he was under a cloud of suspicion. He was in many respects — notably in his passionate devotion to the Saviour—

akin to the great Spanish mystics, although in his early days he had been a disciple of Eckhart, at Cologne. After sixteen years of penances and austere discipline, he abandoned his extreme asceticism, having been warned, he stated, by an angel, to discontinue them. Thereafter, he did not regard these things as impediments to the living of a holy life. His cult was approved in 1381, he himself having died at Ulm in 1365.

The above letter was written to Elspeth Stagal, one of Bl. Henry's spiritual daughters, and brings home the quality and fulness of this most lovable man, the steel-like strength that lay behind his humanity, his wit and humour, perfect manners and undemonstrative holiness, to be judged by its fruits, not its display.

Bl. Raymund of Capua

1300–1399

'THE unity for which members of a religious order are gathered together consists principally in one and the same founder, that is to say (for us) St. Dominic; and in one and the same manner of life, determined by our Constitutions. To assert, therefore, that the brethren who wish to observe this manner of living, and to walk in the footsteps of St. Dominic, are disuniting the Order, is like saying that the soldiers who follow the flag and obey their captain are deserters and bring disunion into the army, even on the very field of battle. It is like saying that the scholars who go willingly to school to hear their master, destroy all study because they separate themselves from those to whom study is displeasing. Oh! if the holy apostles had given way to this fear of causing dissension between Christians and pagans, most certainly they would never have wrought a single conversion. But having realized and understood that the Word of Truth had come to bring, not peace, but the sword of separation between the good and the bad, they did their duty without stopping to consider if any difference of opinion would arise therefrom. In the same way, if Holy Church, who is the assemblage of all the faithful, when she saw one amongst them aspiring to make the vows of religion, had looked upon this separation as bringing disunion into her bosom, she would never have confirmed or allowed the religious orders. It is true that this example rather overshoots the mark, since in our case none of the brethren promise more

16

than the others, the only difference which exists being in the more or less integral manner of observing the common promise: but, it is an arguing from *the greater to the lesser* degree. For, if a certain kind of separation, far greater than ours, has not only not disunited Our Holy Mother the Church, but, on the contrary, confirmed, strengthened and exalted her, how much the less will our Order be divided by the measures I have adopted.

'Do you know who they are who disunite the Order? They are the men who fulfil some of their appointed duties and who disregard others, or who (I mention it with sorrow) fulfil none at all, and belong to the body of the Order without any reason, according to St. Augustine's remark in his Rule: those are the men who disunite and destroy by persecuting the brethren who wish to act differently and to do well. Let us suppose, on the contrary, a hundred persons, accustomed heretofore to do what they please, and now proceeding, little by little, to give up their own and dissimilar wills to follow henceforth the only lawful one; when such is the case, then, and then only, will there be unity of shepherd and flock.'

. . . 'But,' continued the enemies of religious discipline, 'if there is no division properly, of so-called, at least there is always a subject of confusion for those who do not belong to the number of the observant brethren, and whom the public will point at saying: "These are the bad ones; those others are the good."'

'With all due respect,' he replied . . . 'I will show what a poor argument it would be to say: "One of the two is better, *therefore* the other is bad and wicked." We often see in the different houses, brethren who excel in learning and holiness, without, for that reason, holding all the rest to be ignorant and perverse men. But what am I saying! The holiness and learning of the former turn to the honour

17

of the whole Order and of each of its members. That is why we call our holy Doctor St. Thomas in his office: *the honour and glory of the Order of Preachers.* If the Order had a hundred, or two hundred, canonized saints, would not all its members be the more looked up to? Let the eyes of those who recriminate be opened, and let them see that the more perfect individuals there are in a particular species the more perfection will be acquired by the whole, and reversionary interest of this perfection is enjoyed by the individuals who thereby gain greater esteem: a maxim not less true in the moral than in the physical order. To feel jealousy would be (God preserve us from it) to imitate Cain, who was irritated against Abel, seeing him to be more pleasing to God, instead of being irritated against himself for his own wickedness. It would be to imitate Simon the Magician, who wished to possess the graces of the Apostles without embracing the life of the Apostles, and who imagined that he could purchase with money the gifts of the Holy Ghost. . . . Besides, if in spite of all this, there are some who refuse to thus rejoice at the good, the observant brethren, and who complain of finding therein matter for sadness, for such as these, the remedy is simple enough: let them join the good, let them live as they do, and they will be honoured in like manner. This is exactly what we are endeavouring to bring about.'

'. . . We should like,' pursued the adversaries, 'to join your ranks. But this austerity is out of date, especially with these disturbances of the schisms and wars. If you even applied the law pleasantly, it might pass; but you have nothing but harshness and unreasonableness for such of us as wish to try your manner of life.'

'. . . We are told that we should condescend to the weak, dispense from the wearing of serge, allow money to be kept, dispense from attendance in choir, allow meat, and such like things; for thus, many would take up the yoke of observance. We reply: "Fine promises, but no practice!" For, as a matter of fact, in several houses of regular observance, the use of meat is allowed, the fasts are mitigated, the austerity of the rule is tempered, and, nevertheless, none of these men are to be seen there! Moreover, when a house is reformed, all the religious who ask it spontaneously are kept, even if they are infirm and decrepit. In this case they are granted dispensations, and the general austerity is tempered for them up to the time of their death, according to what is demanded by piety and discretion. Why, therefore, do not those who simulate so much good will, and who are quite sure of similar concessions, why, I ask, do they not allow their convents to be reformed, but, on the contrary, become stubborn and resist the Reform with all their might? . . .'

RAYMUND DELLA VIGNE belonged to an important family at Capua and held several important offices in the Dominican Order. By the time he was thirty-seven he was friar at the Minerva in Rome. In 1374 he first met Catherine of Siena and with her his name will be always associated: one of the first things he did when he became her confessor was to allow her to receive Holy Communion as often as she wished. Under Catherine's guidance he was an important messenger to the Papal court at Avignon, during the 'Babylonish Captivity'. Before his death he made several monastic reforms, and to him belongs the credit of the spread of the Third Order. He wrote a life of St. Catherine and died at Nuremberg. He was beatified by Pope Leo XII in the end of the nineteenth century.

The above is a group of extracts from a series of 'Circular Letters' that Bl. Raymund wrote.

St. Bridget of Sweden

1304–1375

PRAISE and honour be rendered to God for all His benefits. My dearest Sir: By that which my Lord and His bishop Alfonsus have told me about you I perceive your good will, which is a sign of particular gifts and graces of the Holy Ghost. May Our Lord give you strength to persevere in it until the end, for His Glory and your salvation. May it not displease you that I write a few lines to give you counsel against the enemy of mankind.

Dear Sir, as I have heard that you are an important and powerful man, and have jurisdiction and authority over others; and as you occupy high places and possess riches and nobility of birth, and the human consolations of wife and children, relations and friends; and as also you are favoured by visits of the Holy Ghost, so it is very necessary for you, dear Sir, to be cautious, and extremely careful to preserve that grace.

*

YOU have also in your letter begged me that I will wholly and fully adopt you as my spiritual son. From my heart I reply that as I do for my own two sons and my daughter, so will I do for you, adopting you as son, that you may be constantly with me enclosed in my heart; that you will be a partaker in my poor prayers and in my pilgrimage. From this pilgrimage across the sea I intend to return as quickly as may be, and immediately I have returned I will let you know.

20

My sons, my confessor, and my daughter commend themselves humbly to you.

*

AS a mother gently welcomes her son who comes to her to beg for her forgiveness, so I say again to him: 'Oh, my son, be converted to me, and I will turn to thee.' Rise up from thy fall and hearken to the counsel of the friends of God. Charity covereth all things, believeth all things, endureth all things, says the apostle. Even though the bridges of friendship be broken down and the friends no longer write to one another as before, yet surely one can send a trifle to that former friend which may be of use to him—a song that may please him or a letter with beneficial rebuke . . . before the Vicegerent of Christ he must acknowledge then on account of his warfare, and his disorder in money matters he had robbed his subjects, broken his oath as a king and the law of the land, and wasted the possessions and wealth of the Crown. There is no other way, but if he follows this path he will become blessed.

ST. BRIDGET was born near Upsala in Sweden. Her father Birger, a prince of the royal blood, was the founder of many churches and monasteries, and both her parents were remarkable for their piety.

In obedience to her father, while still quite young, she was married to Prince Ulpho of Sweden, and became the mother of eight children, one of whom, Katharine, is honoured as a saint. This pious couple enrolled themselves in the Third Order of St. Francis, and ordered their household more after the fashion of a monastery than a palace. After the birth of their children, to break all worldly ties by forsaking their country and friends, they made a painful pilgrimage to Compostella. On their return journey, Ulpho fell ill and received the last Sacraments from the hands of the Bishop of Arras. He was, however, restored to health, in answer to the prayers of his wife, and they reached Sweden, where he died soon after in a monastery of the Cistercian Order, whose severe Rule he was preparing to embrace.

On the death of her husband she felt at liberty to pursue her inclinations as to the manner of life which she desired to live, and renounced the rank of Princess which she held in the world, and entered the monastery of Alvastra. She made many pilgrimages to the Holy Land, to Rome, and elsewhere.

She became the foundress of the Order of Nuns of the Saviour, known as Bridgettines, with the Rule of St. Augustine.

St. Bridget wrote several books which were deservedly popular, especially her book of prayers, *The Sufferings and Love of Christ*.

During the process of canonization, Adam Easton, monk of Norwich and cardinal, wrote a tract in defence of her actions and revelations, and may also have encouraged Abbot Geoffrey of Byland and Richard Lavenham, a Carmelite confessor of Richard II, who did likewise. The other and more influential circumstance was the foundation by Henry V of the Bridgettine house of Syon and the close connexion with Sweden brought about by the Swedish marriage of the Princess Philippa. This led a number of writers to engage upon the task of presenting St. Bridget to their countrymen; one of the first was John Audelay, the poet of Haughmond.

Bridget speaks sternly to kings and Popes and is not afraid. She is 'the Bride of Christ', the chosen instrument of God 'to lay the axe to the root of many an unfruitful tree'. The greatest evil is the world itself; 'there are always the two cities,' writes Jorgensen, 'the two banners of Ignatius, always that Either/Or which was Kierkegaard's cross.' Indeed, Bridget's age is not so far removed from our own and she is 'a saint for our times'.

The Church, after long investigations, has approved *The Revelations* of St. Bridget and has declared that they contain nothing contrary to faith or morals. The future Benedict XIV, referring directly to these Revelations, wrote: 'So far as the instances before us warrant a conclusion, this approbation by no means requires the certitude of faith, but only causes them to be looked upon as probable.' With this in mind, the reader can derive much spiritual profit from the Revelations of the highly favoured Bridget.

The first letter is addressed to King Magnus of Sweden, and the last two to Gomez D'Albornoz in November, 1371.

St. Catherine of Siena

1339–1380

IN the Name of Jesus Christ crucified and of sweet Mary:

Most holy and blessed father in Christ sweet Jesus: your poor unworthy little daughter Catherine comforts you in His precious Blood, with desire to see you free from any servile fear. For I consider that a timorous man cuts short the vigour of holy resolves and good desire, and so I have prayed, and shall pray, sweet and good Jesus that He free you from all servile fear, and that holy fear alone remain. May ardour of charity be in you, in such wise as shall prevent you from hearing the voice of incarnate demons, and heeding the counsel of perverse counsellors, settled in self-love, who, as I understand, want to alarm you, so as to prevent your return, saying, 'You will die.' And I tell you on behalf of Christ crucified, most sweet and holy father, not to fear for any reason whatsoever. Come in security: trust you in Christ sweet Jesus: for, doing what you ought, God will be above you, and there will be no one who shall be against you. Up, father, like a man! For I tell you that you have no need to fear. You ought to come; come, then. Come gently, without any fear. And if any at home wish to hinder you, say to them bravely, as Christ said when St. Peter, through tenderness, wished to draw Him back from going to His passion; Christ turned to him, saying, 'Get thee behind Me, Satan; thou art an offence to Me, seeking the things which are of men, and not those which are of God. Wilt thou not that I fulfil the will of My Father?'

Do you likewise, sweetest father, following Him as His vicar, deliberating and deciding by yourself, and saying to those who would hinder you, 'If my life should be spent a thousand times, I wish to fulfil the will of my Father.' Although bodily life be laid down for it, yet seize on the life of grace and the means of winning it for ever. Now comfort you and fear not, for you have no need. Put on the armour of the most holy Cross, which is the safety and the life of Christians. Let talk who will, and hold you firm in your holy resolution. My father, Fra Raimondo, said to me on your behalf that I was to pray God to see whether you were to meet with an obstacle, and I had already prayed about it, before and after Holy Communion, and I saw neither death nor any peril. Those perils are invented by the men who counsel you. Believe, and trust you in Christ sweet Jesus. I hope that God will not despise so many prayers, made with so ardent desire, and with many tears and sweats. I say no more. Remain in the holy and sweet grace of God. Pardon me, pardon me. Jesus Christ crucified be with you. Sweet Jesus, Jesus Love.

*

IN the Name of Jesus Christ crucified and of sweet Mary:
   Dearest lord and father in Christ sweet Jesus: I Catherine, servant and slave of the servants of Jesus Christ, write to you in His precious Blood: with desire to see you observe the holy and sweet commands of God, since I consider that in no other way can we share the fruit of the Blood of the Spotless Lamb. Sweet Jesus, the Lamb, has taught us the Way: and thus He said: 'Ego sum Via, Veritas et Vita.' He is the sweet Master who has taught us the doctrine, ascending the pulpit of the most holy Cross. Venerable father, what doctrine and what way does He give us? His

way is this: pains, shames, insults, injuries, and abuse; endurance in true patience, hunger and thirst; He was satiate with shame, nailed and held upon the Cross for the honour of the Father and our salvation. With His pains and shame He gave satisfaction for our guilt, and the reproach in which man had fallen through the sin committed. He has made restitution, and has punished our sins on His own Body, and this He has done of love alone and not for debt.

This sweet Lamb, our Way, has despised the world, with all its luxuries and dignity, and has hated vice and loved virtue. Do you, as son and faithful servant of Christ crucified, follow His footsteps and the way which He teaches you: bear in true patience all pain, torment, and tribulation which God permits the world to inflict on you. For patience is not overcome, but overcomes the world. Be, ah! be a lover of virtue, founded in true and holy justice, and despise vice. I beg you, by love of Christ crucified, to do in your state three especial things. The first is, to despise the world and yourself and all its joys, possessing your kingdom as a thing lent to you, and not your own. For well you know that nor life nor health nor riches nor honour nor dignity nor lordship is your own. Were they yours, you could possess them in your own way. But in such an hour a man wishes to be well, he is ill; or living, and he is dead; or rich, and he is poor; or a lord, and he is made a servant and vassal. All this is because these things are not his own, and he can only hold them in so far as may please Him who has lent them to him. Very simple-minded, then, is the man who holds the things of another as his own. He is really a thief, and worthy of death. Therefore I beg you that, as The Wise, you should act like a good steward, made His steward by God; possessing all things as merely lent to you.

The other matter is, that you maintain holy and true justice; let it not be ruined, either for self-love or for flatteries, or for any pleasing of men. And do not connive at your officials doing injustice for money, and denying right to the poor: but be to the poor a father, a distributer of what God has given you. And seek to have the faults that are found in your kingdom punished and virtue exalted. For all this appertains to the divine justice to do.

The third matter is, to observe the doctrine which that Master upon the Cross gives you; which is the thing that my soul most desires to see in you: that is, love and affection with your neighbour, with whom you have for so long a time been at war. For you know well that without this root of love, the tree of your soul would not bear fruit, but would dry up, abiding in hate and unable to draw up into itself the moisture of grace. Alas, dearest father, the Sweet Primal Truth teaches it to you, and leaves you for a commandment, to love God above everything, and one's neighbour as one's self. He gave you the example, hanging upon the wood of the most holy Cross. When the Jews cried 'Crucify!' He cried with meek and gentle voice: 'Father, forgive those who crucify Me, who know not what they do.' Behold His unsearchable love! For not only does He pardon them, but excuses them before His Father! What example and teaching is this, that the Just, who has in Him no poison of sin, endures from the unjust the punishment of our iniquities!

Oh, how the man should be ashamed who follows the teaching of the devil and his own lower nature, caring more to gain and keep the riches of this world, which are all vain, and pass like the wind, than for his soul and his neighbour! For while abiding in hate with his neighbour, he has hate by his side, since hate deprives him of divine charity. Surely he is foolish and blind, for he does not see

27

that with the sword of hate to his neighbour he is killing himself.

Therefore I beg you, and will that you follow Christ crucified, and love your neighbour's salvation: proving that you follow the Lamb, who for hunger of His Father's honour and the salvation of souls chose bodily death. So do you, my lord! Care not if you lose from your worldly substance; for loss will be gain to you, provided that you can reconcile your soul with your brother. I marvel that you are not willing to devote to this, not only temporal things, but even, were it possible, life itself: considering how great destruction of souls and bodies there has been, and how many Religious and women and children have been injured and exiled by this war. No more, by love of Christ crucified! Do you not reflect of how great harm you are cause, if you fail to do what you can? Harm to the Christians, and harm to infidels. For your strife has obstructed the mystery of the Holy Crusade, and is doing so still. If no other harm than this followed, it seems to me that we ought to expect the divine judgement. I beg you that you be no longer a worker of so great harm and an obstructer of so great good as the recovery of Holy Land and of those poor wretched souls who do not share in the Blood of the Son of God. Of which thing you ought to be ashamed, you and the other Christian rulers: for this is a very great confusion in the sight of men and abomination in the sight of God, that war should be made against one's brother, and the enemy left alone, and that a man should want to take away another person's possessions and not to win his own back again. No more such folly and blindness! I tell you, on behalf of Christ crucified, that you delay no longer to make this peace. Make peace, and direct all your warfare to the infidels. Help to encourage and uplift the standard of the most holy Cross, which God shall demand from you

and others at the point of death—demanding also from you
account for such ignorance and negligence as has been committed and is committed every day. Sleep no more, for
love of Christ crucified, and for your own profit, during
the little time that remains to us: for time is short, and you
are to die, and know not when.

May the flame of holy desire to follow this holy Cross
and to be reconciled with your neighbour, increase in you!
In this wise you will follow the way and doctrine of the
Lamb slain and abandoned on the Cross, and you will
observe the commandments. You will follow the way,
enduring with patience the injuries that have been offered
you; the doctrine, being reconciled with your neighbour;
and the love of God, which you will manifest by following
the most holy Cross in the holy and sweet Crusade. As to
this matter, I think that your brother, Messer the Duke of
Anjou, will undertake the labour of this holy enterprise,
for the love of Christ. There would be reason for self-
reproach did so sweet and holy a mystery remain unful-
filled through you. Now in this wise you will follow the
footsteps of Christ crucified, you will fulfil the will of God
and me, and His commands: as I told you that I wished to
see you observe the holy commands of God. I say no more.
Pardon my presumption. Remain in the holy and sweet
grace of God. Sweet Jesus, Jesus Love.

★

I WENT to visit him of whom you know, whereby he
received such great comfort and consolation that he con-
fessed, and disposed himself right well; and he made me
promise by the love of God that, when the time of execution came, I would be with him; and so I promised and
did. Then in the morning, before the bell tolled, I went to

him, and he received great consolation; I brought him to hear Mass, and he received the Holy Communion, which he had never received since the first. That will of his was harmonized with and subject to the will of God, and there only remained a fear of not being strong at the last moment; but the measureless and inflamed goodness of God forestalled him, endowing him with so much affection and love in the desire of God, that he could not stay without Him, and he said to me: 'Stay with me, and do not abandon me, so shall I fare not otherwise than well, and I shall die content'; and he leaned his head upon my breast. Then I exulted, and seemed to smell his blood, and mine too, which I desire to shed for the sweet Spouse Jesus, and, as the desire increased in my soul and I felt his fear, I said: 'Take heart, sweet brother mine, for soon shall we come to the nuptials; thou wilt fare thither bathed in the sweet blood of the Son of God, with the sweet name of Jesus, which I wish may never leave thy memory, and I shall be waiting for thee at the place of execution.' Now think, father and son, how his heart lost all fear, and his face was transformed from sadness to joy, and he rejoiced, exulted, and said: 'Whence comes such grace to me, that the sweetness of my soul should await me at the holy place of execution?' See, he had reached such light that he called the place of execution *holy*, and he said: 'I shall go all joyous and strong, and it will seem to me a thousand years till I come thither, when I think that you are awaiting me there'; and he spoke so sweetly of God's goodness, that one might scarce sustain it. I awaited him, then, at the place of execution; and I stayed there, waiting, with continual prayer, in the presence of Mary and of Catherine, Virgin and Martyr. But, before he arrived, I placed myself down, and stretched out my neck on the block; but nothing was done to me, for I was full of love of myself;

then I prayed and insisted, and said to Mary that I wished for this grace, that she would give him true light and peace of heart at that moment, and then that I might see him return to his end. Then was my soul so full that, albeit a multitude of the people was there, I could not see a creature, by reason of the sweet promise made me. Then he came, like a meek lamb, and, seeing me, he began to laugh, and he would have me make the sign of the Cross over him; and, when he had received the sign, I said: 'Down! to the nuptials, sweet brother mine, for soon shalt thou be in eternal life.' He placed himself down with great meekness, and I stretched out his neck, and bent down over him, and reminded him of the blood of the Lamb. His mouth said nought save *Jesus* and *Catherine*; and, as he spoke thus, I received his head into my hands, closing my eyes in the Divine Goodness, and saying: *I will.*

CATHERINE BENINCASA, the daughter of a tradesman, lived to be the guide and guardian of the Church in one of the darkest periods of its history. As a child in a little steep street in Siena, prayer was her delight. She would say the 'Hail Mary' on each step as she mounted the stairs, and was granted in reward a vision of Christ in glory. This was the first of many visions. When seven years old, she made a vow of virginity, and afterwards endured bitter persecution for refusing to marry and was the household drudge. Our Lord gave her His heart in exchange for her own, communicated her with His own hands, and stamped on her body the print of His wounds. At the age of fifteen she entered the Third Order of St. Dominic, but continued to reside in her father's shop, where she united a life of active charity with the prayer of a contemplative saint. From her home she was summoned to defend the Church's cause. Armed with Papal authority, and accompanied by three confessors, she travelled through Italy, reducing rebellious cities to the obedience of the Holy See, and winning souls to God.

Pope Gregory must have been equally alarmed though not as

much surprised when the wool-dyer's daughter appeared from her Tuscan home—a long and arduous journey in those days—told him that she smelt the stink of the sins that flourished in the Papal court, and by the sheer force of her personality, practical sense, and virtue drove him back to the See of St. Peter where he rightfully belonged. Thus, even though Catherine had not succeeded in permanently ending the Great Schism, and although her achievement could in no way be accounted as dramatic in its finality as the achievement of St. Joan of Arc, she had at least sent one Pope in the right direction.

She was the means of restoring Pope Gregory XI to Rome, and pacifying the tumults in Florence. She had most wonderful ecstasies, and it was said that no one had speech with her without receiving spiritual good. Catherine died in 1380; her relics are in the church of the Minerva, Rome, and her head is enshrined at Siena.

The first letter was addressed to Pope Gregory XI who was then at Avignon; the second to the King of France (Charles V); and the third to Fra Raimondo, describing the end of the young noble of Perugia, unjustly doomed to die by the government of Siena.

St. Vincent Ferrer

To our most holy Lord, Benedict XIII, Pope, Brother Vincent Ferrer, Preacher, a useless servant in regard to both preaching and actions, places himself at the feet of His Holiness.

The Apostle Paul, after fulfilling the mission entrusted to him in preaching the gospel, constrained by revelation, went up to Jerusalem to confer with Peter and the rest. As he himself tells us in the Epistle to the Galatians (Ch. 2): 'Then after fourteen years, I went up again to Jerusalem with Barnabas, taking Titus also with me. And I went up according to revelation and communicated to them the gospel which I preach among the Gentiles; but apart from them who seemed to be something, lest perhaps I should run or had run in vain.' The Apostles also returned from their God-given mission of preaching, in which they had diligently exercised themselves, and 'coming together unto Jesus, related to Him all the things they had done and taught,' as we read in the sixth chapter of the gospel according to Saint Mark. Therefore, in this present letter, I am explaining in all sincerity, to Your Holiness, Christ's Vicar on earth, and the successor of Saint Peter, what I have preached for so long throughout the world, especially in regard to the time of Antichrist and the end of the world; and I do this the more willingly because Your Holiness has so affectionately commanded me to do so.

Concerning these matters I have, in my sermons, been accustomed to draw four conclusions.

The first of these is that the death of Antichrist and the end of the world will occur at the same time. The shortness of the duration of the world after the death of Antichrist has led me to this conclusion, for nowhere in the whole Bible or in the writings of the Doctors can I find a longer period assigned by God for the repentance of those whom Antichrist has seduced than forty-five days after his death.

We read in the Prophecy of Daniel (Ch. 12): 'And from the time when the continual sacrifice shall be taken away and the abomination of desolation shall be set up, there shall be a thousand two hundred and ninety days. Blessed is he that waiteth and cometh unto one thousand three hundred and thirty-five days.' Now, according to the gloss and the commentaries of the Doctors, the first number, to wit, one thousand two hundred and ninety days, equivalent to three and a half years, is the period during which Antichrist reigns as king. Now forty-five is the number which must be added to this to make one thousand three hundred and thirty-five days, and so this number—forty-five—is understood by the Doctors to refer to the duration of the world after the death of Antichrist.

Some people, certainly, are dubious about this, and for two reasons. In the first place they raise the question as to whether the number forty-five refers to solar days or days of a year's duration, since in some passages of Scripture a day is meant to signify a year. But I can see no reason for this being the case in the instance under consideration, since both numbers occur in the same connection, and it is hardly likely that one should stand for annual and the other for solar days. For the Scripture text (Ezekiel Ch. 28) manifestly implies that after the death of Antichrist—elsewhere called Gog—there will not be a year before the end.

Other people are doubtful as to whether the duration of the world after the death of Antichrist be not longer than forty-five days since the Scripture does not expressly deny this. But as the Bible does not mention any determinate time other than forty-five days, it seems unreasonable to suppose that there should be more than forty-five days after the death of Antichrist. If people argue that in so short a time his death could not be published throughout the world in order that the nations might be converted and do penance, some answer that this period of forty-five days will not begin until after the death of Antichrist has been published. Others argue that God, who has ordained that number of days to enable people to repent, will suddenly, either by means of angels or through some terrible portent, make known to the whole world the death of Antichrist.

The second conclusion I draw is that until Antichrist is actually born, the time of his birth will be hidden from mankind. This conclusion is supported by two texts of holy Scripture: the first in the gospel of Saint Matthew (Ch. 24), where His disciples ask Christ: 'Tell us when these things shall come to pass, and what will be the sign of Thy coming and of the end of the world?' Later in the same chapter Christ answers: 'The day and the hour no man knoweth, nor the angels.' The second text is in the Acts (Ch. 1), where the disciples ask the same thing and say: 'Lord, wilt Thou at this time restore the Kingdom of Israel?' And Christ answers: 'It is not for you to know the times nor the moments.' These words must be carefully weighed: 'It is not for you to know the times nor the moments.' It is as if one were to say to the Spanish army and its allies: 'It is not your concern to know the time nor the day when there will be war in Tartary or Armenia, since you have no interests in these places which

35

would make such knowledge pertinent.' But on the contrary, it is most vital for the Tartars and Armenians, themselves, even the peasants, to know the time of such a war so that they may be forewarned.

So, even though there were the most illuminating revelations of the divine Wisdom concerning these matters, it was not necessary for the Apostles and Doctors of the first ages of the Church to know the time of the coming of Antichrist and the end of the the world; but after his birth it is expedient for men, even though they be sinners, or so ignorant as to know nothing of the Apostles and Doctors, to know of this birth, so that they may be forewarned and prepared. This is in accordance with the wisdom, mercy and knowledge of God, who from the beginning of the world was accustomed to send messengers to warn men of any great tribulation about to come to pass. Noah was warned before the deluge, Moses before the liberation of Israel, Amos before the destruction of Egypt, and so on. The Saints, Dominic and Francis, and their respective Orders are warned before the coming of Antichrist and the end of the world, since of both of them the liturgy says that they are supposed to precede the destruction of the world.

The truth of this conclusion demonstrates the falsity of two opinions. One is the dictum that the same length of time ought to pass after the Incarnation until the end of the world, as elapsed from the creation to the Incarnation. Exponents of this opinion base it on the words of Habacuc (Ch. 3): 'O Lord, Thy work is in the midst of the years, bring it to life. In the midst of the years Thou shalt make it known; when Thou art angry Thou wilt remember mercy.'

But this is not in accordance with the gospel texts just quoted, for, since the Doctors agree that the length of time from the creation to the Incarnation was known to the prophets, the Apostles and the Church of God, if it is true that the Incarnation is midway between the beginning and the end, it follows that the time of the end of the world will also be known. This verse of Habacuc should be understood, not of the middle years of the world, but of any human life which, according to Psa. 89, commonly lasts for seventy years.

And so the middle years of a man's life will be about the age of thirty-three, the age at which Christ suffered. For Our Lord did not will to die as a little one by the hand of Herod, neither did He intend to die in old age, but in the midst of His life; that is at the time of the greatest virility. And so, in this way, in the midst of the years, God gave life to His work by the death of His Son and made known the work of His mercy, since before that time He was angry with the human race. In this sense, Isaias, speaking in the person of Christ, says: 'I have said in the midst of my days I will go down into hell.' For Christ, dying in the flower of His manhood, straightway descended into hell (limbo) for the liberation of the just.

Or if the words of Habacuc are taken to mean the middle years of the world's existence, the term does not here imply an equality between the preceding and subsequent times, but should be understood as the middle of interposition. For although the destruction of human life took place in the beginning of time, yet its reparation should not be withheld until the end of time, but should take place between these two terminals. The blessed Gregory uses this mode of speaking when he says that Christ rose from the dead in the middle of the night, since He rose at dawn which stands between the beginning of night and its end, that is by interposition not equality.

Others say that there will be as many years from the birth of Christ to the end of the world as there are verses in the psalter. Thus the exponents of this theory suggest that the first verse of the first psalm *Beatus vir* is a prophecy of the first year after the Nativity, and the second verse a prophecy of the second one and so on. This opinion, however, must be rejected like the first, as it has no foundation except in presumption of heart.

The third conclusion to which I have come is that the coming of Antichrist and the end of the world are near. We may draw this conclusion from the revelation made to the two Saints, Dominic and Francis, and also to many others when these two patriarchs came before the Sovereign Pontiff to ask for the confirmation of their Orders. There is, for instance, the incident of the three lances with which Christ threatened the destruction of the world, as we read at greater length in the histories of these two saints. If the words of Christ and of His Blessed Mother are well studied, these three lances for the destruction of the world are: first, the persecution of Antichrist, second, the destruction of the world by fire, third, the Last Judgment.

The same conclusion is reached with more exactitude by studying the revelation made to Saint John in the Apocalypse (Ch. 20): 'I saw an angel coming down from heaven, having the key of the abyss and a great chain in his hand, and he seized the dragon, the old serpent, who is the devil and Satan, and bound him for a thousand years, and after that he must be loosed for a short time.' The ordinary gloss explains this shutting up and binding chiefly by the death of Christ on the Cross and His descent into hell, and reckons a thousand years to mean a multitude of years, taking the determinate to signify the indeterminate, that is that a thousand years is looked upon as signifying the whole time from the death of Christ to the coming of

Antichrist, when Satan will be loosed for the temptation and seduction of mankind. Nevertheless, this binding of Satan may be very properly understood of his binding, lest he should have tempted or seduced the nations by means of the persecution of the faithful under the Roman emperors. This binding occurred in the time of the blessed Pope Sylvester when Constantine became a Christian and gave the Church her patrimony. For, from that time until the founding of the Orders of Franciscans and Dominicans is a thousand years, and after that Satan must be loosed. According to this theory, the Angel descending to bind Satan is held to be Pope Sylvester, or rather Christ acting through him.

There are several opinions which run contrary to this conclusion. One affirms that there will be a drought of forty years duration before the end of the world. This is untenable because in that case the burning of the world would come about as a natural consequence of the exceeding dryness. For, as the deluge did not occur in the ordinary course of events, but through a divine judgment, so also this deluge of fire will be a direct outcome of the divine power; for, according to the Doctors, it will find men living in great prosperity and the world in a state of tranquility, and, according to Saint Jerome, the fire will burn all matter, even water and the sea.

Others affirm that Elias and Enoch will come before the advent of Antichrist, in order to preach and to warn men against his deceptions. This is false, as may be seen from the Apocalypse (Ch. 11), where it is said of the followers of Antichrist: 'And the holy city they shall tread under foot two and forty months. And I will give unto my two witnesses, and they shall prophesy a thousand two hundred and sixty days in sackcloth.' Now, Elias and Enoch, properly speaking, will not come before the advent of

Antichrist, but at the same time, as it is evident both from the text and the gloss that he had already begun to reign.

Others affirm that the gospel signs ought to precede the coming of Antichrist. According to Saint Luke: 'There shall be signs in the sun and in the moon,' etc. These signs, however, properly speaking, will occur after the death of Antichrist and immediately before the judgment.

Another objection is that Jerusalem and the Holy Land will be conquered by the Christians before the coming of Antichrist. Many texts from the Prophet Ezechiel (Ch. 32), and the acts of the Martyr Methodius, seem at first sight to imply that, at the advent of Antichrist, the Holy Land will be in the hands of Christians. But this conquest has already been partially realized by Christian princes, notably by Godfrey de Bouillon; nor does it appear that the numbers and disposition of Christians are such as to enable them to carry the conquest to its conclusion. In fact, the text of Saint Luke (Ch. 21) seems to contradict this: 'Jerusalem shall be trodden under foot by the peoples, until the times of the nations shall be fulfilled.' The words of Ezechiel and Methodius should be understood more in the light of an allegory of the Church Militant and its numbers than of the Holy Land and its provinces.

Again we are told that all nations will be brought to the one Catholic Faith before the coming of Antichrist. This does not seem to be true, for this conversion will rather take place after the death of Antichrist when, seeing themselves to have been deceived by his falsehoods, men will return to the unity of the Faith. See Ezechiel (Ch. 39): 'I have given thee to the wild beasts, to the birds, and to every fowl and to the beasts of the air to be devoured,' speaking of the death of Antichrist—Gog—'and I will set my glory among all nations; and they shall see my judgment, that I have executed and my hand that I have laid upon them.'

Another opinion affirms that the gospel of Christ must be preached throughout the world before the coming of Antichrist, according to the text of Saint Matthew (Ch. 24). 'And this gospel of the kingdom shall be preached in the whole world, for a testimony to the nations; and then shall the consummation come.' This text is subject to diverse methods of exposition according to the manifold general preaching of the gospel throughout the world. First it was preached by the Apostles to every creature according to the precept of Christ in the last chapter of Saint Mark. This precept was fulfilled in the time of the Apostles as is shown in the Epistle to the Colossians (Ch. 1): 'In the word of truth, the gospel which has come to you, as also it is in the whole world and bringeth forth fruit and groweth.' And towards the end of the same chapter: 'The gospel which you have heard which is preached to all creation which is under heaven.' And in Romans (Ch. 10): 'Their sound is gone forth unto all the earth.' Then came the consummation of the Jewish people and the destruction of Jerusalem under Titus and Vespasian. In the second place the gospel has been preached and is still being preached daily by the Dominicans and Franciscans. And after this, straightway will come the consummation and destruction of the world by Antichrist and his followers. The third preaching of the gospel throughout the world will take place after the death of Antichrist by certain faithful ones of each nation, who will have been wonderfully preserved by God for the conversion of the rest; and then will come the last consummation of the world.

The fourth conclusion I have drawn is that the time of Antichrist and the end of the world will take place in a short space of time, a mercifully short space of time and exceedingly quickly. This conclusion, although in substance it is found in the first homily of Saint Gregory, nevertheless, strictly and properly speaking, I prove it in many different ways.

First, from the revelations made to Saints Dominic and Francis, which I have spoken of previously. By this revelation it is made manifest *that the whole duration of the world rests on a certain conditional prolongation obtained by the Virgin Mary in the hope of the correction and conversion of the world by the aforesaid Orders.* For Christ said to the Blessed Virgin: 'Unless the world is corrected and converted by means of these Orders I will no longer spare it.' Since, therefore, the conversion and correction of the world has not followed but rather the reverse, for greater crimes and wickedness abound, and, it must be regretfully admitted, these Religious Orders themselves, who have been given for the conversion and correction of the world, are in reality so moribund and relaxed that little religious observance is kept in them, the observant man must admit that this conclusion is amply proved.

In the second place the same conclusion is drawn from a certain other revelation (a most certain one to my mind), made just over fifteen years ago to a religious of the Dominican Order. This religious was very ill indeed and was praying lovingly to God for his recovery so that he might again preach the word of God as he had been wont to do with great fervour and ardour. At last, while he was at prayer, these two saints appeared to him as in a dream, at the feet of Christ making great supplication. At length, after they had prayed thus for a long while, Christ rose and, with one on either side, came down to this same religious lying on his bed. Then Christ, touching him caressingly with the finger of His most holy hand, gave him a most definite interior comprehension that, in imitation of these saints, he must go through the world preaching as the Apostles had done, and that He, Christ, would mercifully await this preaching for the conversion and correction of mankind, before the coming of Antichrist. At once, at the touch of Christ's fingers the aforesaid religious rose up entirely cured of his sickness.

As he diligently followed the apostolic mission divinely committed to him, Providence, in testimony of the truth, gave this religious, not only numerous signs as he had given Moses, but also the authority of the divine Scriptures as he had given John the Baptist since, because of the difficulty of this mission and the slight weight of his own unaided testimony, he was greatly in need of help. Hence, of the three divine messengers sent to men by divine Providence under the name of angels, many persons believe him to be the first, of whom John has written : 'And I saw another angel flying through the midst of heaven having the eternal gospel to preach to them that sit upon the earth and over every nation and tongue and tribe and people, saying with a loud voice: "Fear the Lord and give Him honour, because the hour of His judgment is come. And adore ye Him that made heaven and earth, the sea and the fountain and the waters. Let him who is able understand."'

Since then the aforesaid religious has been travelling for thirteen years over the world, and is still journeying, preaching every day and in many labours, and though he is now an old man, more than sixty years old, he still holds this conclusion as most certain. . . .

The same conclusion is also shewn me by another revelation which I heard from a certain holy and devout man —as I consider him. When I was preaching in the province of Lombardy for the first time eleven years ago, there came to me from Tuscany a man sent, as he said, by certain most

43

holy hermits of great austerity of life, to tell me that a divine revelation had been made to several of these men that the birth of Antichrist had already occurred, and must be announced to the world so that the faithful might prepare themselves for so dreadful a combat, and so they had sent the aforesaid hermit to me that I might tell the world. If then, as appears from these revelations, it is true that Antichrist had already completed nine years of his accursed life, then it follows that my conclusion is also true.

Another clear revelation which I heard while in Piedmont, told me by a Venetian merchant on whose word I can rely, confirms this conclusion. He was beyond the seas in a certain convent of the Friars Minor, and was attending Vespers on a certain feast day. At the end of Vespers, two little novices, according to their custom, singing the 'Benedicamus Domino,' were visibly rapt in ecstasy for a considerable period of time. At length they cried out together: 'Today, at this hour, Antichrist, the destroyer of the world is born.' This struck those present with fear and amazement, and among those who actually heard it was the Venetian who told me of the occurrence. When I questioned him and made enquiries about this event, I found that it happened nine years previously, and so this is further corroboration of what I have already said.

This same conclusion is further borne out by many other revelations made to many other devout and spiritual persons. For, travelling as I do, through many regions, provinces, kingdoms, cities and towns, many devout and spiritual persons come to me, referring with certitude to the coming of Antichrist and the end of the world, which they have received in many and very diverse revelations, and in all of these there is the greatest concord.

Innumerable demons, forced to a confession of the truth

44

have said the same thing. In many parts of the world, I have seen many persons possessed by the devil, who were brought to one of the priests of our company for exorcism. When the priest began to exorcise them they spoke openly of the time of Antichrist, in accordance with what has already been said, crying out loudly and terribly so that all the bystanders could hear them, and declaring that they were forced by Christ and against their own will and malice, to reveal to men the truth as given above, so that they might save themselves by true penance. These revelations have the effect of leading to contrition and penance the numerous Christians standing round. But when the demons are questioned, or even conjured to tell the truth of the birth place of Antichrist, they will not reveal it. . . .

From all that has been said above, I hold the opinion, which I think to be well founded, though not sufficiently proven for me to preach it, that nine years have already elapsed since the birth of Antichrist. But this I do preach with certitude and security, the Lord confirming my word by many signs, that in an exceedingly short time will come the reign of Antichrist and the end of the world.

Our Lord Jesus Christ, foreknowing that this doctrine will be unacceptable to carnal persons and the lovers of this world, said in the Gospel of Saint Luke (Ch. 17): 'And it came to pass in the days of Noah, so shall it also be in the days of the Son of Man. They did eat and drink and they married wives and were given in marriage, until the day that Noah entered into the ark, and the flood came and destroyed them all.' The same thing happened in the days of Lot: they ate and drank, they bought and sold, they planted and built. On the day that Lot left Sodom it rained fire and brimstone from heaven and all were des-troyed. This will happen on the day when the Son of

45

Man shall be revealed. On that day, whoever is on the roof and his vessels in the house must not come down to take them, and he who is in the field must not return to his house. Remember Lot's wife!

Again in the First Epistle to the Thessalonians (Ch. 5) we read: 'And the times and moments, brethren, you need not that we should write to you; for you yourselves know perfectly that the day of the Lord will come as a thief in the night. For when they shall say peace and security; then shall destruction come upon them, as the pains of her who is with child. And they shall not flee.'

This, most Holy Father, is what I am preaching concerning the time of Antichrist and the end of the world, subject to the correction and determination of Your Holiness, whom may the Most High preserve.

July 7th, 1412.

VINCENT, born at Valencia, in Spain, of a respectable family, showed the gravity of old age, the Roman Breviary tells us, even when quite a child. Considering within himself, as far as his youthful mind knew it, the dangers of this dark world, he received the religious habit of the Order of Preachers when he was eighteen years of age. After his solemn profession, he diligently applied himself to sacred studies, and gained, with the highest honours, the degree of theology. Shortly after this, he obtained leave from his superiors to preach the word of God. He strove against the unbelief of the Jews, and refuted the false doctrines of the Saracens, with so much earnestness and success, that he brought a great number of infidels to the faith of Christ, and converted many thousand Christians from sin to repentance, from vice to virtue. For God had chosen him to teach the way of salvation to all nations, and tribes, and tongues; as also to warn men of the coming of the last and dread day of judgment. He so preached that he struck terror into the minds of all his hearers, and turned them from earthly affections to the love of God.

His mode of life, whilst exercising this office of apostolic preaching, was as follows: every day he sang Mass early in the morning; every day delivered a sermon to the people; and, unless absolutely obliged to do otherwise, he always observed a strict fast. He gave holy and prudent advice to all who consulted him. He never ate flesh-meat, or wore linen garments. He reconciled popular strife, and restored peace to kingdoms that were at variance. He zealously laboured to restore and maintain union in the seamless garment of the Church, which at that time was rent by a great schism. He shone with every virtue, and treated his revilers and persecutors with meekness and affection, walking ever in simplicity and lowliness.

St. Bernardine of Siena

1380–1444

WHENEVER I meditate on what the Scripture says of fraternal sympathy and tenderness, I feel the sword of sorrow pierce my soul to the quick, and it is in vain that I try to restrain my tears. . . . He, thanks to whom I could in all places give myself to the Lord, has been taken from me, and my heart is broken because of it. I do my best to master my grief, but I acknowledge my failure to do so. For I must give vent to the sorrow which gnaws at my heart. I must speak of my grief in order that compassionate hearts may afford me some little comfort.

You know, my very dear brethren, how justified is my lament, how piteous my wound. You know how faithful was the companion who has forsaken me on my pilgrimage, how vigilant was his care, how great his love of work and sweetness of character. He was, moreover, greatly attached to me and loved me with all his soul. In religion he was a beloved brother to me, and in the greatness of his love he was as another self. Pity me, I beseech you, and bemoan my fate. Weak in body, I was often ill, when he would support me and lead me by the hand. When I grew faint-hearted he never failed to encourage me, when indolent and careless over the things of God he would spur me onwards, when heedless or forgetful he was there to reprove me. Why hast thou been taken from me, Vincent? Why hast thou been torn from me, thou who wast ever one with me, thou who wast after my own heart? Is there anyone who would have been unmoved at the sight of so

48

sweet a link in a mutual love? Is there another save death, the enemy of all happiness, that would not have spared us?

Why, I wonder, did we love each other, and why, in that case, were we separated? A hard plight, not for thee, but for me. For, my brother, if thou hast quitted dear friends, thou hast, I verily believe, found those dearer still. Instead of poor and puny me, thou now rejoicest in the sight of God and joinest in the choir of angels without grief for my absence. But I, what do I find in thy stead? How happy were I to know whether thou still rememberest me, thy faithful friend, tottering under the weight of trials and bereft of thy support, the staff of my weakness! I long to know whether, in the midst of an abyss of light and plunged in eternal felicity, it is still given thee to think of the miseries of this world. Thy love, I know, has not diminished. It has only changed, since the sight of God cannot have made thee forgetful of us. For does not God Himself take care of us? Thou hast rejected that which is infected with weakness, but charity has never yet destroyed that which is holy. Ah! do not ever forget me, do not separate thyself from me. Thou knowest where I crawl, in what place I lie, and where thou hast left me. There is now no one to help me. In the path of life I turn mine eyes, as I was wont, towards my brother Vincent, and he is there no more. In my misery I groan like a man destitute of help. Who shall I question in my perplexity? To whom in adversity shall I give my confidence? Who will assist me to carry my burden? Who will remove danger from my path? For was not Vincent ever wont to precede my steps? You who knew him know how true are my words. Was not thy heart, Vincent, better acquainted with my wants than I myself? Did it not feel my griefs and pains more acutely? In thy loving and bashful manner didst thou not often correct the asperity of my sermons, tempering with thy friendship the fire thereof?

The Lord had, moreover, endowed him with such a fluency and pregnancy of language that he was able to preach without any preparation. He astonished all by the wisdom of his advice and counsels, as regards both domestic and other affairs. He hastened to meet visitors to prevent their intruding on my repose, permitting only those whom he could not pacify to have access to me, and sending others on their way. He was nowise engrossed in his own affairs, but entered into the least of my cares and made all my concerns his own, in order to give me more leisure, since, in his modesty, he deemed my leisure to be more fruitful than his; and yet the more he devoted himself to others the less gratitude did he receive, so that he who thus spent himself in his neighbour's service was not infrequently in want of the necessaries of life, of food, of clothing and a proper resting-place. I thank thee from the bottom of my heart, sweet friend, for the fruits of my preaching and labour during the course of my journeys in Italy, since, if I have been useful in anything, if my teaching has been salutary, it is to thee that I owe it. For whilst thou attended to domestic affairs, I was either resting, thanks to thee, or else delivering my sermons. How could I have been otherwise than secure when my interests lay in thy keeping, thou, my right hand, the apple of my eye, thou, my very heart and tongue? How many faults might I not have committed in the course of my preaching if his upright intelligence, his enlightened mind and his great discernment had not directed me with so much zeal and solicitude! . . . In my Order, I confess, I found no other master to teach me how to preach the word of God. . . . If there is any good in me, I owe it to thee. . . .

May the tears flow and fall in torrents from my wretched brow, so that they may, perchance, suffice to wipe out the stain of my crimes, of those crimes which have incurred the Divine wrath against me. . . . Many of those who were at the funeral of my beloved brother were astonished to see the tears gush from my eyes, tears coming straight from the heart. In vain I forced myself to conceal my grief. In the attempt, the fire which was consuming my heart only shot up into brighter flames which ravished my soul. And it crept with so much suppleness and nipped with so much cruelty that it succeeded at last in wringing tears from my eyes. In my lamentations, I deplore nothing of what the world regrets. I grieve for a salutary adviser, a faithful helper in the things of God. I grieve for Vincent—Vincent my faithful companion during the twenty-two years and more in which I have preached the gospel. . . . What a wretched being am I! Parted from my better half, I wallow in the mire, and am asked if I weep! My heart is broken, and I am asked whether I feel any grief! I weep and am grieved because my strength is not that of a rock and because my flesh is not of brass! I suffer and pity myself, 'and my sorrow is ever before me'. I cannot boast Jeremiah's insensibility when he said: 'Thou hast smitten them and they have not uttered one complaint.'

BERNARDINE was born at Massa, on 8th September, 1380. At the age of three he lost his mother, and at the age of six his father. He was brought up by his mother's sisters and his cousin: women remarkable for their piety. He grew up under their care and seems to have been peculiarly susceptible to their religious influence. When he was seventeen years old the plague fell on Siena, he volunteered to minister to the sick, persuaded twelve companions to do the same, and after four months of exhausting labour caught the disease himself. On his recovery he resolved to enter the religious life, and, after hesitating between the Franciscans and the Dominicans, chose the former. Then he studied and became a priest, quietly absorbed in the routine of the house until the discernment of his Superior discovered that his vocation was to be a preacher.

Illness overtook him; he knew that he was dying. In the convent his brethren gathered round his bed to hear his last words. Then, as his life was fading away, he gave his brethren a sign to lift him and place him upon the ground. And there, with his arms extended in the sign of the Cross, he died.

He was particularly eloquent when preaching on the Holy Name of Jesus. He was also responsible for the revival of discipline among the Franciscans, and from 1438 to 1442 he was Vicar-General of the Order. Six years after his death he was canonized. In art he is represented holding to his breast the monogram of the Sacred Name.

His hearers were not only for the moment affected and melted into tears, but in many instances a permanent regeneration of heart and life seemed to have taken place through his influence. Those who had defrauded made restitution; those who owed money hastened to pay their debts; those who had committed injustice were eager to repair it. Enemies were seen to embrace each other in his presence; gamblers flung away their cards; the women cut off their hair and threw down their jewels at his feet. Wherever he came, he preached peace; and the cities of Tuscany, then distracted by factions, were by his exhortations reconciled and tranquillized, at least for a time. Above all, he set himself to heal, as far as he could, the mutual fury of the Guelphs and the Ghibellines, who at that period were tearing Italy to pieces.

From the contents of the above letter, it would appear to have been addressed to some religious.

St. Colette

1381–1447

JESUS! Dearest and best beloved mothers, daughters, and sisters, as right humbly as I can and may in God, I most heartily recommend my poor soul to your good prayers and devout intercessions before our Saviour; desiring your complete health of soul and body, and begging you most lovingly to struggle on with all your might to become good and perfect religious, by grafting all your works on to the root of deep humility; kindling in your hearts an ardent love of God, and serving Him with care and humble devotion; fully observing the holy rule, by loyally rendering up all that you have freely vowed and promised; and resisting to the end the temptations and seductions of the devil.

Though you be weak and feeble, yet the enemy in hell has no power to overcome you, if you do not will it so. And, moreover, be patient in all your trials and set-backs, for we always benefit and bear fruit more abundantly in times of pain and sorrow than ever we do when things go well and we are comforted. For if there be a true way that leads to the Everlasting Kingdom, with never any fear of leading astray, it is most certainly that of tribulation and persecution patiently suffered.

Now, concerning those daughters that you mention in your letter, I have written to the Mother Abbess explaining to her my intentions. [I recommend my mode of writing to the Flamangues. (?)] I humbly recommend to you, my poor brother P. I beseech the Holy Spirit that he may ever deign to keep you in his holy grace.

S. COLETTE

THREE hundred and sixty years after her death at Ghent, Colette Boillet was canonized. Born at Carbeil in Picardy, a carpenter's daughter, she tried her vocation with the Beguines and the Benedictines, but failed. Next she became a recluse at Corbie and eventually revived the Franciscan spirit among the Poor Clares. Her plan was blessed by Peter de Luna. She soon became Superioress of the whole Order and her reform spread far and wide— France, Germany, and Flanders. Her chief devotion was to our Lord's Passion and her supreme attraction to the practice of holy poverty.

She was at first a Franciscan tertiary who lived as an anchoress beside her parish church. In 1406 she set out to walk to Nice to lay before Peter de Luna (who was acknowledged as Pope in France) her scheme for the reform of the Poor Clares. He was so impressed that he made Colette Superioress of the whole Order with full powers to carry out the reform. This she proceeded to do by visiting all the convents in France, Savoy, Flanders, and Germany: some adopted her suggestions, others received her with contumely. In addition she founded seventeen new convents and some friaries. She also associated herself with St. Vincent Ferrer in his efforts to heal the schism in the papacy. Colette exercised a notable influence over people of rank, like James of Bourbon and Philip the Good of Burgundy. All men spoke of the beauty of her person and character, of her humility and sweetness. St. Colette died 6th March, 1447.

St. John of Capistrano

1386–1456

O KING, give heed, I pray you. This is a time of crisis. The Christian faith is assailed by impious foes, and Christian blood is copiously shed, and will, we fear, be shed yet more and more. If help be not speedily forthcoming, the enemy will vanquish us all. I pray you, therefore, and, by the Blood of our Lord Jesus Christ, I beseech that you will lend your powerful aid. Join with the other princes who have been moved to take action, and of whom many have promised to go in person with their forces. Your majesty has generals who are excellently qualified for such an expedition, likewise the bravest and most robust of men. With such a host, and your abundant wealth, your highness could with God's help, and if you were so minded, yourself crush this ferocious Mohammed. Set yourself, then, mighty ruler, with brave heart to this task; and in this manner show your courage, your religion, your zeal for the faith, your love of God. Thus will all the world behold in you a truly Christian king, sparing not your gold nor life itself in the defence of the Christian faith.

*

I DO not tell all this, Holy Father, to show that I have done anything important, for I am of no account; but, that your Holiness may know my unswerving fidelity to you, and may be assured that I have set aside all other considerations so as to labour, feeble though I be, for the overthrow of the enemies of Christ and the faith. And, truly, Holy Father, all other things must be ignored, and all our energies directed against this mighty foe that has sworn utterly to efface the Christian name; for, although many believe that great things have been accomplished in this diet, to me it seems that nothing, or almost nothing, has been done.

ST. JOHN was born at Capistrano in the diocese of Sulmona, in the Abruzzi, on 24th June, 1386. When he had finished his studies he took the degree of a doctor of laws at Perugia. In 1412, King Ladislas of Naples appointed him governor of Perugia. During the war with the Malatesta faction he was imprisoned for meddling in politics. In 1416, after his release, he took the habit of St. Francis. Influenced by St. Bernardine, he became a famous preacher in 1425, spreading the devotion to the Holy Name of Jesus throughout Italy. In 1426, he was appointed papal inquisitor; as such he most energetically combated the Jews and the Fraticelli; he also promoted a reform in his own Order, which was adopted by the general chapter in 1430. In 1431, he was elected Minister General of the Observants; as Apostolic Commissary and Visitor he was sent to Venice, to the Holy Land, to Milan, to France and to Sicily. Invited by Frederic III, he preached the crusade in Austria, Bavaria, Poland, and Silesia (1451); he also attempted to reconcile the Hussites of Bohemia and Moravia. He urged the Christian princes to go to war against the Turks at the diets of Frankfort and Wiener-Neustadt. In 1455, he entered Hungary at the head of a Christian army and, with the famous General Hunyadi, won the great victory of Belgrade, 14th July, 1456. He died of a fever contracted at Illok (Ujlak) near Peterwardein. He was beatified by Leo X and canonized in October, 1600 (4th June, 1724). He has been called 'champion of the Holy Name, scourge of the Hebrews, destroyer of heresies and commander of the Catholic armies against the infidels'. He was famed for his fiery eloquence which attracted such crowds that, when it was announced that he would preach in Brescia, the magistrates laid in a large store of food for the influx of people and provided a guard of forty men to save John from being crushed by the concourse of 10,000 people who had assembled in the market place before sunrise.

St. John was a prolific writer, and his works are all directed against the heresies of his day. The first letter was addressed to King Henry VI of England, and the second the Pope.

St. Joan of Arc

1412–1431

✠ JHESUS MARIA ✠

KING OF ENGLAND, and you, Duke of Bedford, who call yourself Regent of the realm of France, you, William de la Pole, Earl of Suffolk, John Talbot, and you, Thomas, Lord Scales, who call yourselves lieutenants of the said Bedford:

Submit to the King of Heaven; surrender to the Maid who has been sent by God the keys of all the good cities which you have taken and violated in France. She has come by God's order to restore the royal blood. She is ready to make peace, if you will submit, provided that you quit France and pay for what you have taken. And you, archers, gentlemen, soldiers of whatever rank before Orléans, depart in God's name into your own country; and if you will not, expect soon to see the Maid, who will inflict great damage upon you.

King of England, if you fail to do as I ask, I am a military chieftain and, in whatever place in France I come upon your men, I shall cause them to depart, whether by their will or no; and if they refuse to obey I shall have them killed. I am sent here by God the King of Heaven to meet them body to body and drive them out of the realm of France. But if they will yield I will grant them mercy. And doubt it not, for you shall not have the realm of France from God, the King of Heaven, son of Saint Mary, but it will be held by Charles, the true heir, for God wishes it and has so revealed to him by the Maid, and he will enter Paris with a noble company.

If you will not believe the tidings sent you from God and the Maid, we shall strike you down in whatever place we find you, and make you such a great 'hahay' as has not been seen in France for a thousand years unless you submit to us. And know well that God will lend such strength to the Maid that you will be unable to withstand her and her good soldiers.

You, Duke of Bedford, the Maid begs and requires of you that you do not seek your own destruction. If you consent you will be able to come in her company, thence where the French will perform the noblest deed ever done for Christianity. Answer, if you will make peace in the city of Orléans; and if you refuse, you will remember it to your sorrow.

AN illiterate, seventeen-year-old peasant girl rode to Chinon and changed the history of France. In her native Domrémy, in Lorraine, Jeanne d'Arc was as adept at milking cows, ploughing and sewing as she was at seeing visions and hearing 'voices'—Saints Catherine, Margaret, and Michael, and even the Archangel Gabriel. Impelled by these 'voices', Jeanne had come to the court of the Dauphin Charles with her schemes for driving out the English, then occupying a good part of France, and for conquering the Burgundians, allies of the English.

What manner of maid was she? Voltaire found her a conquering hero with not too many morals; Schiller changed her into a furious romantic, dying on a battlefield; Anatole France saw her as a tool of the medieval Church and of military strategists in Charles' army; Mark Twain sentimentalized her as pure, beautiful and discreetly maidenly; it was left to Shaw to make her the first modern woman. The safest estimate of her character is that she was a little of each—headstrong, presumptuous, crafty in battle, deeply religious. That she was beautiful, romantic, is fiction; that she was chaste not even her judges doubted.

Considering the condition of France under the slothful and weak-willed Charles VII, it is little wonder that she, a sturdy peasant girl, was listened to. Had not Merlin, the Sibyl, and Bede prophesied such a one? So Joan, accompanied by such famous knights as Dunois and Gilles de Rais, later notorious as Bluebeard, set out to raise the siege of Orléans, her first objective. What she did not know was that she was starting a spirit of nationalism and patriotism.

Rumours spread in advance of the small army of the strange girl, clothed in white, astride a black horse, who carried an axe but conquered by prayers. Villages capitulated without struggle. Before raising the siege of Orléans, Joan dictated the above demand for the surrender of the English who were besieging the city—a letter which later at her trial was supposed to prove her a heretic.

The English scoffed and called her a sorceress. But their derision was premature, for Joan, with small forces, routed the English. In the words of the Duke of Bedford, this success was 'caused of unleyefulle doubte that thei hadde of a Desciple and Lyme of the Feende called the Pucelle (Maid) that used fals Enchauntments and Sorcerie'.

Three months afterward, on 17th July, 1429, Joan had Charles crowned King of France at Rheims. But the coronation proceedings gave the English time to fortify Paris, import more troops, and solidify positions, and when Joan once more rode forth it was to defeat. Finally, in May, 1430, she was captured at Compiègne by the Burgundians. Charles VII, with customary treachery, now that he had no further use for her, made no attempt to ransom her. Sold to the English for 10,000 pieces of gold, she was turned over to the Bishop of Beauvais as a heretic and witch.

Before fifty or sixty jurists and theologians, with seventy charges against her—hearing voices, seeing visions, dressing in male attire, putting the sign of the cross and the names of Jesus and Mary on her letters, blasphemy—she was tried and found guilty of twelve charges. A high paper crown on her head, with the words 'Heretic, Relapsed, Apostate, Idolater', she was burned at the stake on 30th May, 1431. They took her charred body out of the flames when her clothes had been burned off, to show that she was really a woman. To prevent her cult from ever pervading France, they scattered her ashes into the Seine—a useless precaution. She was canonized in 1920.

St. John Fisher

1459–1535

IF this is true [that a brother marry the wife of his brother deceased without children], and I have no doubt that it is most certainly true, who can deny, considering the plenitude of power which Christ has conferred on the Sovereign Pontiff, that the Pope may dispense, for some very grave reason, for such a marriage?

Even if I granted that the reasons on either side were evenly balanced, and that the difficulties on each side could be solved with equal ease, I should nevertheless be more inclined to give the power of dispensation to the Pontiff, for this reason that the theologians of both sides grant that it belongs to the plenitude of the pontifical office to interpret ambiguous places of Holy Scripture, having heard the judgement of theologians and jurists. Otherwise to no purpose Christ would have said: 'Whatsoever thou shalt loose on earth shall be loosed in heaven, and whatsoever thou shalt bind on earth shall be bound in heaven.' Now, as it is most evident that by their very acts the Sovereign Pontiffs have more than once declared that it is lawful in the case mentioned to dispense in favour of the second brother, this alone would powerfully move me to give my assent, even if they alleged no reasons or proofs. From these premises no scruple of hesitation remains in my mind about the matter. I wish your eminence long life and happiness.

MAY, 1527

*

AFTER my most humble commendations, where as ye be content that I should write unto the king's highness, in good faith I dread me that I can not be so circumspect in any writing but that some word shall escape me wherewith his grace shall be moved to some further displeasure against me, whereof I would be very sorry. For as I will answer before God, I would not in any manner of point offend his grace, my duty saved unto God, whom I must in everything prefer. And for this consideration I am full loth and full of fear to write unto his highness in this matter. Nevertheless, sithen [since] I conceive that it is your mind that I shall so do, I will endeavour me to the best that I can.

But first here I must beseech you, good Master Secretary, to call to your remembrance that at my last being before you and the other commissioners for taking the oath concerning the king's most noble succession, I was content to be sworn unto that parcel concerning the succession. And there I did rehearse this reason, which I said moved me, I doubted not but the prince of any realm, with the assent of his nobles and commons, might appoint for his succession royal such another as was seen unto his wisdom most according; and for this reason I said, that I was content to be sworn unto that part of the oath as concerning the succession. This is the very truth, as God help my soul at my most need. Albeit, I refused to swear to some other parcels by cause that my conscience would not serve me so to do.

Furthermore, I beseech you to be good master unto me in my necessity. For I have neither shirt nor sheet, nor yet other clothes that are necessary for me to wear, but that be ragged and rent to shamefully. Notwithstanding I might easily suffer that, if they would keep my body warm. But my diet also, God knoweth how slender it is at many times, and now in mine age my stomach may not away but with a few kinds of meats, which if I want I decay forthwith, and fall into coughs and diseases of my body, and can not keep myself in health. And as our Lord knoweth, I have nothing left unto me to provide any better, but as my brother of his own purse layeth out for me to his great hindrance. Wherefore good Master Secretary eftsoons [forthwith] I beseech you to have some pity upon me, and let me have such things as are necessary for me in mine age and especially for my health.

And also that it may please you by your high wisdom to move the king's highness to take me unto his gracious favour again, and to restore me unto my liberty out of this cold and painful imprisonment; whereby ye shall find me to be your poor beadsman for ever unto Almighty God, who ever have you in his protection and custody.

Other twain things I must also desire upon you: that one is that it may please you that I may take some priest within the Tower by the assignment of master lieutenant to hear my confession against this holy time; the other is, that I may borrow for the comfort of my soul. This I beseech you to grant me of your charity. And thus our Lord send you a merry Christmas and a comfortable to your heart's desire.

At the Tower, the 22nd day of December.

Your poor Beadsman,

Jo. Roffs.

JOHN FISHER was born at Beverley in 1459 the son of a draper, and educated at Cambridge, in which University he held several important offices, and was eventually elected Chancellor. He was also confessor to Margaret, Countess of Richmond, the mother of Henry VII, and was her adviser and agent in her many works of pious munificence, especially in the foundation of St. John's and

Christ's Colleges at Cambridge. In 1504 Fisher was consecrated Bishop of Rochester, one of the poorest dioceses of the kingdom.

In 1534 all officials were required to swear to a form that the marriage of Henry and Catherine was illegal and invalid. This Bishop Fisher could not conscientiously do, though he professed himself willing to swear allegiance to the succession of the children of Anne Boleyn. During his detention in the Tower, he was subjected to various cruelties. It was during this interval that the Pope conferred upon him a cardinal's hat. On hearing this the King declared that the Pope might send the hat, but he would take care the Bishop had no head to fit it on. Henry VIII had declared himself to be Supreme Head of the Church in terms which have never been claimed by any of his successors; and the King's Solicitor-General, in a private conversation with Fisher, extracted from him, in an unguarded moment, an admission that he did not accept the King's claim of Supreme Headship over the Church. His trial and condemnation soon followed.

The martyr's head was struck off at a single blow, and his venerated body, after being for a while exposed to the populace, was hastily buried in Barking churchyard, from which it was afterwards removed, and interred, with that of Sir Thomas More, within the Tower. His death was lamented all over Europe, and several Sovereigns, in their letters, expressed their disapprobation of the King's cruelty. Seldom had fidelity been repaid with more injustice, love with more bitter hate. Fisher laboured for the furtherance of learning in this country; he was the friend of Erasmus and the great promoters of Greek in England.

The second letter was written to Thomas Cromwell, as secretary of King Henry VIII, after the Bishop had been eight months in prison, i.e., on 22nd December 1534.

St. Thomas More

1478–1535

WE are in the greatest sorrow and danger.
Multitudes are dying all round us. Almost everyone in
Oxford, Cambridge and here in London has been ill
lately and we have lost many of our best and most honoured
friends; among them—I grieve at the grief I shall cause you
in relating it—our dear Andreas Ammonius, in whose
death both literature and all good men suffer a great loss.
. . . In this 'sweating sickness' no one dies except on the
first day of attack. I myself and my wife and children are
as yet untouched, and the rest of my household has recovered. I assure you there is less danger on the battlefield
than in this city. Now, as I hear, the plague has begun to
rage in Calais, just when we are obliged to land there on
our embassy—as if it were not enough to have lived in the
midst of the contagion, but we must follow it also. But
what would you have! We must bear our lot. I have
prepared myself for any event.

★

I DO not know which to admire the most, your modesty
in willingly laying down an office of such dignity and
power, your unworldliness in being able to despise it, or
your integrity, having no fear of resignation; but, with
many other men, I give to your act my most cordial
approval, as certainly most excellent and wise. Indeed I
can hardly say how heartily I congratulate you on your

singular good fortune and how I rejoice in it for your sake, for I see you retiring far away from the affairs of the world and the bustle of courts, raised to a rare eminence of fame, both on account of the honourable manner in which you have held your office and the honourable way in which you have resigned it. Happy in the consciousness of duty well done, you will pass your time quietly and peacefully in literature and philosophy. Whilst daily I appreciate more and more the happiness of your lot, I realize my own misery, for although I have no business worth mentioning, yet my attention is fully occupied, for poor talents find even trivial things as much as they can manage. I have so little free time that I can rarely visit you, or excuse my remissness in writing—indeed I have scarcely been able to get ready this present letter.

Herewith I would beg your grace to accept a little book [Utopia] . . . relying on the ready kindness with which you welcome all works of fancy, and trusting to the favour I have always experienced from you. Thus I hope that even if the book pleases you but little, yet your good will may extend to the author. Farewell, my Lord Archbishop.

*

THE Bristol merchant brought me your letters the day after he left you, with which I was extremely delighted. Nothing can come from your workshop, however rough and unfinished, that will not give me more pleasure than the most accurate thing anyone else can write. So much does my affection for you recommend whatever you write to me. Indeed, without any recommendation, your letters are capable of pleasing by their own merits, their wit and pure Latinity.

There was not one of your letters that did not please me

extremely; but to confess frankly what I feel, the letter of my son John pleased me most, both because it was longer than the others, and because he seems to have given to it more labour and study. For he not only put out his matter prettily, and composed in fairly polished language, but he plays with me both pleasantly and cleverly, and turns my own jokes on myself wittily enough. And this he does not only merrily, but with due moderation, showing that he does not forget that he is joking with his father, and that he is careful not to give offence at the same time that he is eager to give delight.

Now I expect from each of you a letter almost every day. I will not admit excuses—John makes none—such as want of time, the sudden departure of the letter-carrier, or want of something to write about. No one hinders you from writing, but on the contrary, all are urging you to do it. And that you may not keep the letter-carrier waiting, why not anticipate his coming, and have your letters written and sealed, ready for anyone to take? How can a subject be wanting when you write to me, since I am glad to hear of your studies or of your games, and you will please me most if, when there is nothing to write about, you write about that nothing at great length! This must be easy for you, especially for the girls, who, to be sure, are born chatterboxes, and who have always a world to say about nothing!

One thing however I admonish you: whether you write serious matters or the merest trifles, it is my wish that you write everything diligently and thoughtfully. It will be no harm if you first write the whole in English, for then you will not have much trouble in turning it into Latin; not having to look for the matter, your mind will be intent only on the language. That, however, I leave to your own choice, whereas I strictly enjoin you, that whatever you have composed, you carefully examine before writing it out clean, and in this examination first scrutinize the whole sentence, and then each part of it. Thus, if any solecisms have escaped you, you will easily detect them. Correct these, write out the whole letter again, and even then examine it once more, for sometimes, in re-writing, faults slip in again that one had expunged. By this diligence your little trifles will become serious matters, for while there is nothing so neat and witty that may not be made insipid by silly and inconsiderate chatter, so also there is nothing in itself so insipid, that you cannot season it with grace and wit if you give a little thought to it.

Farewell, my dear children.

From the Court, the 3rd September.

*

OUR Lord bless you, good daughter, and your good husband, and your little boy, and all yours, and all my children, and all my God-children, and all our friends. Recommend me when ye may, to my good daughter Cecily, whom I beseech our Lord to comfort. And I send her my blessing and to all her children, and pray her to pray for me. I send her an handkercher: and God comfort my good son her husband. My good daughter Daunce hath the picture in parchment, that you delivered me from my lady Coniers, her name is on the back-side. Show her that I heartily pray her that you may send it in my name to her again, for a token from me to pray for me. I like special well Dorothy Colley, I pray you be good unto her. I would wit whether this be she that you wrote me of. If not yet I pray you be good to the other as you may in her affliction, and to my good daughter Joan Aleyn too. Give her I pray you some kind answer, for she sued hither to me this day to pray you be good to her. I cumber you good Margaret much, but I would be sorry, if it should be any longer than tomorrow. For it is Saint Thomas even, and the octave of Saint Peter: and therefore tomorrow long I to go to God: it were a day very meet and convenient for me. I never liked your manner toward me better, than when you kissed me last: for I love when daughterly love and dear charity hath no leisure to look to worldly courtesy. Farewell my dear child, and pray for me, and I shall for you and all your friends, that we may merrily meet in heaven. I thank you for your great cost. I send now my good daughter Clement her algorism stone, and I send her and my godson and all hers, God's blessing and mine. I pray you at time convenient recommend me to my good son John More. I liked well his natural fashion. Our Lord bless him and his good wife my loving daughter, to whom I pray him to be good as he hath great cause: and that if the land of mine come to his hand, he break not my will concerning his sister Daunce. And our Lord bless Thomas and Austin and all that they shall have. . . .

THOMAS MORE was the son of Sir John More, one of the Justices of the King's Bench. He was born in London in the year 1480, and was educated with great care, first at a school in the City, and afterwards at the University of Oxford. He then studied law at New Inn, when he was admitted Barrister and appointed Public Lecturer, having from the commencement of his course given proof of those great talents and that virtuous life for which he was ever afterwards so conspicuous. The great success of More in his profession attracted the attention of Henry VIII, who called him to the Court, and, for many years, showed him every mark of confidence and favour, finding the greatest pleasure in his learned and witty conversation. He conferred on him the honour of knighthood, chose him for many important employments, and finally, on the fall of Cardinal Wolsey, nominated him High Chancellor of England. Moreover, the King would visit him privately at his house in Chelsea, and spend long hours in his company.

More was twice married, and had a family to whose education he devoted all possible care.

His reverse of fortune began with the question of the King's divorce, and was completed by that of the Royal Supremacy in things spiritual. Seeing the course events were taking, he thought it best to retire from public life, and obtained leave to resign the Chancellorship. This reduced him to poverty, as he had never availed himself of the opportunities he had had of acquiring wealth; but this was a real cause of joy to him, and never was he more cheerful than when he talked with his family on their change of fortune. His fidelity to his conscience in the matter of the Supremacy was the cause of his being sent to the Tower for fifteen months. Sentence was pronounced against him, but his execution was deferred for a while, and every effort was made to shake his constancy. The 6th of July, 1535, was the date fixed for his execution.

'If we had been master of such a servant,' said the Emperor Charles V, 'we should rather have resigned the best city in our dominions than have lost such a worthy counsellor.' His many writings are held in high esteem. He was canonized in 1925.

The first letter was written to Erasmus, in August, 1517. The second was addressed to Archbishop Warham, on the occasion of his resigning from the office of Lord Chancellor; Thomas More intimates that the post was given up by Warham's own wish, and there is no hint that Wolsey, his successor, ousted him from it. The third letter was to his dearest children and to Margaret Gigs, whom he numbered among his own. The last letter was written to his daughter, the day before his execution; it breaks off abruptly at the end, and was the last thing he ever wrote.

Allusions in this last letter have been explained as follows: Dorothy Colley was Margaret Roper's maid and friend; she married More's secretary, John Harris, and was living at Douai when Stapleton wrote, and supplied him with many details about More. Joan or Jane, Aleyn: another maid of Margaret Roper's. 'Saint Thomas even and the octave of Saint Peter' is the eve of the feast of the Translation of St. Thomas of Canterbury (7th July) and octave-day of the Feast of SS. Peter and Paul (29th June). Margaret Clement's 'algorism stone' was for arithmetic: apparently a slate. The 'natural fashion' of John More was his manner of asking his father's blessing. 'Thomas and Austin' (Augustine) were the two sons already born to John More. (Stapleton, Hallet's edition, p. 203.)

St. Thomas of Villanova

1488–1555

V ERY HOLY FATHER,

It is not without fear and dismay that I have received the letters by which your Holiness constitutes me Archbishop of Valentia. For where is the man who, regarding with the eye of faith the weight of this high ministry, would not tremble and be cast down at the sight of so holy and responsible a dignity! May the very good and merciful Jesus Christ our Lord help me to serve His Church, for which He descended from heaven, to found and cement it with the blood that He and His saints have shed! As it is not in my power worthily to express the gratitude which I feel for the kindness with which it has pleased your Holiness to honour me, I will at least show it in part by my conduct, acquitting myself faithfully of the office imposed on me. For I believe your Holiness is never so well pleased as when you see those whom you have called to share in your solicitudes, zealous in assisting you to govern that flock that God has committed to your care, to rule, govern, and increase it. This is assuredly my intention and resolution. May God grant that I may be able to execute it as I desire. As to the rest, I have nothing which is not yours, and which you have not acquired by the benignity your Holiness has shown me. I assure you there is no one in the world more ready than myself to render you submission and obedience in whatever it shall please you to command me. I have taken the oath of fidelity before consecration, according to custom, and I have sent it you, as you commanded in your letter.

May God keep and preserve your Holiness many years for the good and peace of His Church.

From your Holiness's

Humble and devoted creature,

Father Thomas of Villanova.

THOMAS was born in Castile. He was brought up in a devout household, and was given a liberal education. After receiving his degree, he was appointed professor of philosophy in the university of Salamanca, but in 1518 he gave up this post of academic distinction to become a simple Augustinian friar. Ordained to the priesthood two years later, he began a life of evangelical fervour which won for him the title of 'Apostle of Spain'.

He rose almost immediately to offices of responsibility in his Order, and those who had the care of the government of the Church began to cast covetous glances in his direction. He managed, however, to evade the burdens of ecclesiastical administration until 1544, when he became Archbishop of Granada. The Emperor Charles V had been asked to nominate someone for this see, and in a conference with his secretary about it, the name of Thomas was suggested, but the suggestion dismissed, as the Emperor was sure he would decline the honour. The secretary, however, misunderstood the direction given, and wrote the name of the saint in the documents which were being prepared. When he would have corrected it, the Emperor said, 'No, let it stand. I see the hand of God in this mistake.'

Granada had not in centuries seen such a bishop. The chapter of the cathedral gave him 4,000 ducats with which to furnish his house. He received them with great gladness, but immediately sent them off to be given to the poor. He visited every corner of his diocese with incessant devotion, preaching, administering the Sacraments, relieving the poor, consoling those in trouble, ministering to the sick and dying, and all with a sweetness that won every heart.

73

The revenues of his diocese were large, but he kept practically nothing for himself, giving away everything with a lavish but not injudicious hand. He constantly exhorted the wealthy noblemen and burghers to be richer in mercy and charity than in worldly goods. 'If you desire God to hear your prayers', he would say, 'do you hear the voice of the poor. If you desire God to forestall your wants, forestall those of the suffering without waiting for them to importune you.'

The above letter was addressed to Pope Paul III.

St. Cajetan

1480–1547

M Y REVEREND MOTHER,

If the waters of the celestial wine are abundantly watering your heart, according to my hopes, the torrents escaping from that inexhaustible fountain will extinguish the ardour of the flames that are consuming mine, and will cause me to know, like you, when receiving the adorable Body of Jesus Christ, the enchanting sweetness of a fire that purifies while it enlightens. In this dark vale of tears, in this solitary place of exile, I wish solely to feed upon this secret manna, this delicious substance; and all that is pleasant in the world to the rest of the children of Adam will for me have only bitterness. Never, no never shall I lose the recollection of the charity that animates you, in approaching the Holy Table. O what happiness for me, if I then obtained your prayers! Without doubt they would prevail with your Bridegroom not to disdain mine. They would cause me to be heard at last through your beneficent mediation. Plead therefore with Him for a soul which the darts of the cruel enemy of His salvation have pierced and deeply wounded. Do not refuse the succour of your prayers, either to my mother according to nature, whom you should regard as your sister, or to the friend dear to my heart, whom you should regard as your son, because I regard him as my brother. I commend to you also the city of Rome, once so holy, and even now enriched with the relics of so many martyrs; but which nevertheless resembles, through the wicked conduct of its inhabitants, impious Babylon. I have just offered, sinner as I am, the sacrifice of the Lamb without spot in one of the splendid temples that adorn the city, in the very chapel where are now carefully preserved the lance that pierced the Saviour's side, and the image known under the name of Veronica. O may I gather the fruit, and feel the efficacious virtue of these holy relics! May I profit by the consoling expressions of your letter, which I shall have always present to my recollection, and for which I shall never cease to render thanks to your Spouse!—I am, reverend mother, your son in Jesus Christ.

CAJETAN was born in Lombardy, Italy, in 1480, of noble parentage. From childhood, he was known as 'The Saint'; and, while still young, he left his native town to seek obscurity in Rome, but was forced to accept office at the court of Julius II. There existed at this time among the noble families of Rome a Confraternity of Divine Love, the objects of which were the keeping alive of the Divine Love in the hearts of its members, and mutual support against temptation. Cajetan joined this community, and inspired it with his own burning enthusiasm. At this time, even devout Christians rarely communicated more than three or four times in the year. Cajetan urged that this was an abuse; that the soul needed more frequent nourishment; and, at his exhortation, many became monthly, and even weekly, communicants. The death of his mother necessitated his return to Vicenza, where, in spite of the opposition of his family, he joined a confraternity of poor labourers, whose object was much the same as that of the Society of the Love of God, of which he had been so zealous a member in Rome. His earnest, loving exhortations stimulated the zeal of their humble souls, and many were seen communicating at the altar thrice in the week. He also undertook the charge of a hospital of incurables, and many other works of mercy. All his charitable schemes prospered. But his Director, seeing that his enthusiasm and abilities demanded a wider sphere than the little town of Vicenza, removed him to Venice, and afterwards to Rome.

The state of the Church in Rome excited in Cajetan the deepest distress. To renew the lives of the clergy, he, in company with three other leading members of the Congregation of the Love of God, instituted the first community of regular clerks, known as Theatines, one of whose most distinguished members was Laurence Sempoli, the author of the *Spiritual Combat*. They devoted themselves to preaching, the administration of the Sacraments, and the careful performance of the Church's rites and ceremonies. When the Germans, under the Constable Bourbon, sacked Rome, Cajetan was scourged, to extort from him material riches which he did not possess. Soon after, he was sent to Naples, to found there a House of his Order. His fervour for souls in Naples was so remarkable, that he obtained the name of the soul-hunter, 'Venator animarum'.

Worn out at last with toil, sickness, and disappointment, Cajetan died on 7th August, 1547, at Naples. He was canonized in 1671.

This letter was written to Laura Mignani (a Holy Cross sister) from Rome on 31st July, 1517, in the first year of St. Cajetan's priesthood. It evidently reflected some kind of personal crisis he was experiencing.

Bl. John Forest

1473–1538

M OST Serene Lady and Queen, my daughter most dear in the bowels of Christ, I received your letters by the hands of your young servant Thomas, and when I read them I was filled with incredible joy, because I saw how great is your constancy in the Faith, of your holy Mother the Church. In this, if you persevere, without doubt you will attain salvation. Doubt not of me that by any inconstancy I should disgrace my grey hairs. Meanwhile I earnestly beseech you that you would steadfastly pray for me to God, for whose spouse we suffer torments, to receive me into His glory. For it I have striven these four and forty years that I have passed in the Order of St. Francis. Now that I am in my sixty-fourth year I am no longer necessary to the people; wherefore I desire to be dissolved and to be with Christ. Meanwhile do you keep free from the pestilent doctrine of the heretics, so that if ever an angel should come down from Heaven and bring you another doctrine from that which I have taught you, you must give no credit to his works but reject him; for if he should teach you another doctrine, he does not come from God.

These few words you must take in lieu of consolation: but that you will receive from our Lord Jesus Christ, to whom I specially commend you, to my Father Francis, to St. Catherine; and when you hear that I am being executed, I heartily beg of you to pray for me to her. With these words I beg you farewell. I send you my rosary as I have but three days to live.

IF Father John Forest was, as surmised, sixty-four at the time of his martyrdom, he must have been born in 1473. At the age of seventeen he entered the Franciscan monastery at Greenwich, and some nine years later studied at the House of his Order at Watergate, Oxford, where he probably took his Doctor's degree, as he is styled by that academic distinction in his last disputation. He was, no doubt, already sufficiently distinguished for learning and general abilities, for in January, 1525, he was deputed by Cardinal Wolsey to preach at Paul's Cross, a comminatory sermon reminding his brethren, the Franciscans, that all religious under solemn vows who left their monastery without due permission incurred the penalty of excommunication. In 1526-7, Fr. Forest received the post of confessor to Queen Catherine of Aragon, who herself became so much attached to the Order that she expressed a wish to be buried in one of the Franciscans' churches.

22nd May, 1538, witnessed the curious spectacle of a Franciscan friar going to Smithfield to suffer both for *treason* in maintaining the Pope's spiritual supremacy, and apparently for *heresy* in not formally abjuring what was actually a Lutheran perversion of the teaching of the Catholic Church on the subject of sin and its punishment. The burning of the martyr over a slow fire near the St. Bartholomew's Spital Gate was witnessed by a vast concourse, including the Lords of the Privy Council, the Lord Mayor and Aldermen of London, and the high nobility in town. Latimer—unforeseeing his own subsequent fate—preached the dying sermon, but was reminded by Forest that he himself had held very different opinions about the Pope's authority years before! He ended by exclaiming: 'Open thou thine eyes, take example from that Holy Bishop of Rochester and the Blessed Thomas More, who renounced the goods of this world and chose rather to die than to lose their immortal souls.'

Fr. Forest was suspended from a gibbet and slowly burnt to death. He refused to draw his feet from the fire when the flames mounted up, but said many prayers in Latin, the last being the *Domine miserere mei*.

This letter was addressed to Catherine of Aragon, wife of King Henry VIII.

St. Ignatius of Loyola

1491–1556

OBLIGED as I am to dispatch immediately some of my companions to the Indies, to Ireland, and to Italy, I cannot write to you at such length as I should wish to do. The bearer of this letter is Master Francis Xavier of Navarre, son of the lord of Xavier, and one of our Company. He goes by order of the Pope, and in accordance with the request of the King of Portugal, besides two others, who are proceeding by water. I must inform you that the ambassador of the King of Portugal, with whom Master Francis travels, is much attached to us, and we owe him a great deal. He hopes to be of service to us, if he can, with his King, and every other person, in all things which concern the service of God our Lord. I beg you, therefore, to receive him with all the courtesy and hospitality you are able. And if Araoz is there, let him take this letter as if his own, and so he will give the same credence to Master Francis at my petition, as he would give to myself.

I beg much to be remembered to the lady of the house, and to all whom the house contains. May Our Lord be ever on your side and be your aid.

Poor in goodness,

IÑIGO

*

YOU must bear in mind that our Lord did not call you to enter His Society, in order that you might lead the life of a hermit and seek your own satisfaction, of how elevated and pure soever a nature. Your vocation compels you to seek to promote the salvation of others, in order thus to imitate the Son of God, Who left the bosom of His Father, in order that He might redeem our souls, that He might give them food, and peace, and life, by means of His own weariness, sufferings, and death. Therefore I exhort and command you to follow so great an Example, so illustrious a Leader, to quit Oñate in order to visit and seek out many persons who are desirous of serving God, and of modelling their households according to the counsel you may give them. You ought to feel persuaded that these journeys will be all the more pleasing to God, because, as I am well aware, they will be anything but pleasing to your natural man. And I have reason to believe that their result cannot fail to be satisfactory.

★

VENERABLE Doña Isabel Roser, my mother and sister in Christ our Lord,—In truth, I would willingly please you, for the greater glory of God, and retain you in spiritual obedience, as hitherto, watching with solicitude for your greater good and the perfection of your soul. But as I have not the necessary strength, because of my continual illnesses, and of being occupied in matters about which I am specially bound to God our Lord, and to his Holiness in God's name—seeing, too, in my conscience, that this least Society ought not to have special charge of matrons bound by vows of obedience, as contrary to the object of this small Society, as I explained about six months since to his Holiness—I have thought it more for God's glory that I should retire altogether from this care, and keep you no longer in obedience as my spiritual daughter, but consider you rather as a good mother, such as you long have been, for the greater glory of God our Lord. And therefore for the greater service, praise, and glory of His Eternal Goodness, I remit you, as far as I can, and without prejudice to higher authority, to the eminently wise judgement and decision and will of his Holiness, so that your soul may be entirely tranquil and consoled, to the greater glory of God.

★

MOST HOLY FATHER,

Your obedient servants, the General and the priests of the Society of Jesus in the Church of Santa Maria della Strada, erected, instituted, and approved in the holy city by your Holiness, cease not with all their strength and their poor ability to devote themselves to the service of the Church of God and of our Lord Jesus Christ, and consequently of your Holiness, His Vicar upon earth. But as these priests are solicited by many considerable persons, particularly in Spain, to take the direction of nuns and of women who desire to serve God piously, and as they are convinced this would be a great obstacle to the other functions they have to fill in God's service, conformably to the chief end of the Institute of your Holiness, and as this responsibility is just commencing, and though a small hindrance in the beginning, may grow greater hereafter, these priests humbly throw themselves at your feet, and ask as a special favour that in their Institution and the confirmation of this Society, which may be regarded as an explicit declaration, and may be so expressed, you may deign to declare that it is a great hindrance to the other duties and service of God which is incumbent on them by your Holiness' chief Institute, that they should undertake

the charge of any nuns or sisters, or of any women whatever, or receive any under vow or obligation of obedience;
and that the Fathers should in no way be bound to undertake this charge, nor is it expedient for their Institute and
Society.

★

'INSTEAD of striving to draw a little blood, *seek* our divine Master Himself in a more direct way, I mean *His very
holy gifts,* such, for instance, as the gift of tears, which
causes you to weep, now for your own sins and those of
your neighbour, now at the spectacle of Our Lord's
mysteries; whether in this life or in the next, now with
love for the Divine Persons'; or again: 'The intensity of
faith, hope, and charity, *joy and spiritual repose,* intense
consolations, the *flight of the spirit,* impressions and divine
illuminations and all other spiritual tastes and feelings
relating to such gifts, like humility. . . . All these very
holy gifts should *be preferred* to all corporal acts [of morti-
fication], which are only good *in so far* as they serve to
acquire these gifts, either wholly or in part. By this I do
not mean to say that we should seek them *solely* for the
pleasure and delectation that we find in them; certainly
not. But recognizing that, without these gifts, all our
thoughts, words, and works are imperfect, cold, and
tarnished, *we should desire these gifts* in order that they may
thereby become righteous, ardent, and bright, for God's
greater service. It therefore follows that *we should desire*
these most precious gifts, either wholly or in part, and
these spiritual graces in so far as we can by their aid procure
greater glory to God.'

IGNATIUS (Iñigo), founder of the Society of Jesus, was born in
1491 in Loyola Castle, near Azpeitia, in the Basque province of

83

Guipuzcoa, Spain, the youngest of the several sons of Beltran Yanez de Onez y Loyola, called Inigo (Lopez de Recalde). The name 'Ignacio' he assumed in 1537, 'Iñigo' disappearing in 1542. Before his conversion he followed the profession of arms and led a worldly life, until he was wounded by a cannon ball during the siege of Pampluna, 20th March, 1521. He was converted by spiritual reading whilst convalescing at Loyola. On his recovery he went to Monserrat, then to Manresa (1522). His experiences in spiritual combat he wrote down in his *Spiritual Exercises*. After a pilgrimage to the Holy Land (1523), he began his studies at Barcelona when thirty-three years old (1524), and continued them at Alcalá, Salamanca, and Paris (1528–35), and in England September 1531, the year Henry VIII was acknowledged Supreme Head of the Church. His idea of founding a society for the greater glory of God brought him into conflict with the Inquisition. At Salamanca, he was imprisoned on suspicion of being one of the mystical sect of the Illuminati (Alumbrados). At Paris, his efforts were successful and on 15th August, 1534, he and six companions took the vows of poverty, chastity, and evangelization of the Holy Land, at St. Denis chapel on Montmartre. Later they spent one year at Venice, and then went to Rome and placed themselves under the direct obedience of Pope Paul III, who gave them a field of labour in Rome. Ignatius was ordained priest at Venice, 24th June, 1537, and after the approbation of the Society of Jesus in 1540, was elected its first General, on 4th April, 1541. He composed the Constitution, 1541–50. Its most important innovations were that he dispensed entirely with the monastic habit, exempted his clerics from all those common devotional exercises by which so much time was consumed in monasteries, and dispensed them from singing their offices together in choir. The members of his Society were to devote themselves to preaching, hearing confessions, giving spiritual exercises, and educating youth. He founded the German College, the Roman College, and two orphan asylums. He never intended to oppose his Society as a bulwark to Protestantism, but it became a stronghold of the Church at the saddest period of her history. Ignatius lived to see his Order divided into twelve provinces with 100 colleges. He died at

Rome on 31st July, 1556, was beatified on 27th July, 1609, and canonized on 12th March, 1622. His body is in the Gesu church in Rome.

9,000 pages of print contain his letters. The first letter printed above was written to his nephew in 1540. The second was to St. Francis Xavier, written in 1552. The third letter was to Isabel Roser, and the fourth a petition to Pope Paul III. The last letter was written to St. Francis Borgia from Rome in 1548, beseeching him to moderate his excessive penances.

St. John of God

1495–1550

YOU have afforded me great consolation by performing so exactly what we agreed upon together respecting the obedience you were to show to Father Portillo in the management of the poor. If you always act in this manner, we shall both of us feel satisfied on this point, whereas if you took your own understanding for a guide, I should have reason to fear the deceits of the devil. I entreat you, my brother, in the name of God, to persevere in the same line of conduct, and to show the same obedience until it shall please our Lord that I should go where you are, and you shall come where I am, for when we are together I am not much afraid of your doing anything at your own suggestion; but when absent from their fathers, children ought to show their deference and obedience to them by not doing anything which might cause them displeasure, but, on the contrary, shall act in such a manner that when they see them again they may have cause to rejoice in the Lord. Since He has employed me to take care of you, and has united us in brotherly union, by His love, let us act together, and by this means you will find that we shall put to flight and conquer the devil. For you love me and wish to obey me, obey Father Portillo, whom I give you as father in my place. Receive all that he shall say to you as if I said it to you, and do all that he should recommend you as if I were recommending it to you, until I see you.

*

MY good Duchess, if we consider carefully this present life we shall see that it is nothing else than a continual warfare as long as we remain in this valley of tears. We are constantly being persecuted by three mortal enemies, the devil, the world and the flesh. The world attracts us by its vices and its riches. It promises us a long life, saying: 'you are young, have a good time, enjoy yourself, it will be time enough to think of repentance when you are old.'

The devil is always setting traps in order to make us fall and to harm us. He tries to prevent us from doing good and being charitable. He inspires us with an exaggerated love of the goods of this world, so that we become forgetful of God and the care which we should have to preserve our soul pure and pleasing in His sight. When we have finished one affair he persuades us to engage in another and always to put off the amendment of our life to a later date. Thus we never manage to escape from the toils of the demon until comes the hour of our death, and then we shall see how false was all that the world and the devil promised us. But the Lord will judge us as He finds us at the hour of our death and, for that reason, it is well to mend our ways in time and not be like those who are always putting it off till tomorrow.

Our other enemy, which is the worst, because it is one that we carry about with us, seeks by flattering attentions to lead us into perdition. This is the flesh, our body, which desires only to eat well, drink well, sleep well, be well dressed, do little work and satisfy all the desires of our carnal nature and of our vanity.

In order to overcome these three enemies, we have need of the grace and of the assistance of Jesus Christ. We must despise self and trust only in Our Lord, confessing our sins humbly at the feet of our confessor, performing the penance imposed on us and resolving never more to sin. If we have the misfortune to sin, we must confess it truthfully. In this way can we hope to overcome the three enemies of which I have spoken. We must not trust in ourselves, otherwise we shall fall into sin a thousand times a day. We must put our trust in Jesus Christ and refrain from sinning for His sake. We must not grumble nor do evil, nor judge our neighbour nor do to him other than what we would have others do to us. Let us desire that all should be saved; and let us love Jesus Christ and serve Him for His own sake and not through fear of hell.

*

THIS letter will give you some idea of how greatly I am afflicted and in want, for which, however, I give thanks to Our Lord Jesus Christ. My dearly beloved brother in Christ, the number of poor people who come here seeking help is so great that I am often astonished how we manage to assist them. But Jesus Christ looks after all and provides them with something to eat. For the wood alone, we need seven or eight ducats a day. The city is so big and it is very cold, particularly at this winter season. . . .

So many poor flock to this house of God. Between bed cases, those who can get around, and attendants, we number more than 110. This being a general hospital, we receive every kind of case. Thus we have cripples, paralytics, lepers, deaf and dumb, insane, those with skin diseases, and old people and children, besides counting many pilgrims and vagrants who call here. To these latter we supply heat, water, salt and other condiments for the food. We have no income for all this, but Jesus Christ provides for everything. Every day it costs four and a half to five ducats to buy meat, flour and wood, not counting medicines and clothing which are an additional expense. When the daily alms do not suffice to meet the expenses, I buy on credit. If I cannot get this, we fast.

In this way I find myself in debt solely for the love of Jesus Christ. I owe more than two hundred ducats to pay for shirts, boots, sheets, woollen blankets and for many other things required in this house of God; also for the upbringing of the babies whose mothers have brought them here. Thus, beloved brother in Jesus Christ, seeing myself so much in debt it often happens that I do not go out of the house. Seeing so many poor people, who are my brothers and equals, in such great necessities either of body or soul and not being able to help them makes me very sad. With all this I place my trust only in Jesus Christ Who will free me from all debts because He knows the secrets of my heart. That is why I say, unhappy the man who puts his confidence in men and not in Jesus Christ. Whether he wills it or not, he will be abandoned by men, whilst Jesus is faithful and constant and provides for all. May all thanks be given to Him for ever, Amen, Jesus.

THIS saint was a shepherd, like so many other holy servants of the Good Shepherd. He had many experiences of life which in one way or another fitted him for the work which God had for him to do in the end. He ran away from his home when a lad, and served in the wars against the Turks. He was over forty years old when, struck with remorse at the thought of his wasted life, he went to North Africa and devoted himself to the work of ransoming the Christian slaves who had been captured by the Moors. Returning to Spain, he devoted himself to helping the sick and the outcast.

One night, the story goes, he found a poor man in the streets, starved, ill, and near to death. He took him in his arms to a shelter, and fetched water to wash his feet when, as he tenderly wiped them with the towel, he was amazed to see that the feet of the beggar were pierced with the marks of nails, radiant with an unearthly brightness. Raising his eyes in awe, he heard a voice which said, 'John, all that thou hast done for the poor in My name, thou hast done unto Me'. And with these words the vision vanished.

St. John devoted his life to a heroic ministry to all who needed his care, and at last he laid it down for another. In 1550, he plunged into the River Xinel to save a child from drowning. The exposure brought on an illness which ended in death. He went to his reward at the age of fifty-five.

The recipients of the above letters are unknown.

Bl. John of Avila

1500–1569

MY dearly loved sister in Christ,
        I look upon the special regard for your soul
with which God inspires me, as a sign of His favour, for not
only does the law of charity require this sympathy from
me, but I hope that my compassion for your sorrows will
ensure me a share in the joy that you are one day to receive
from our Lord's hands. Do not feel miserable about the
state you are in, but rather rejoice in God's love for you,
although you may not realize it at the time. Do not depend
upon your feelings; they are often misled and deceiving.
Neither our confidence in our justification nor our doubts
about it affect the reality. 'I do not judge myself,' said St.
Paul, 'He that judgeth me is the Lord' (1 Cor. iv, 3, 4).
Our folly is so great that it is often best for our souls to
think that God loves but little, or not at all. When we feel
dry, sad, despondent and afflicted, so that we seem to suffer
the torments of hell, our foolishness is more easily kept
within bounds than when we are made presumptuous by
the freedom and happiness which God's consolations are
wont to bring. Like a loving Father, lest His children fall
into negligence and false security, He hides the love He
bears them so that they may always preserve some holy
fear to keep them from becoming negligent and so losing
the inheritance He is keeping for them in the kingdom of
heaven. Watching them and loving them as He does, He
dissimulates His tenderness and keeps them safe by teaching

them his painful lesson, and not only watches in silence but Himself sends more trials and temptations.

After some great sorrow, God usually grants us happiness, as to Abraham He gave 'Isaac the desired', which name signifies 'laughter'. After a while the Almighty plunged the patriarch into grief again, by commanding him to kill the son He had bestowed for his consolation: so does God often deprive His children of their happiness, bidding them sacrifice it and live in sadness. The Apostles felt perfectly safe and confident as they embarked with Christ in their boat; yet they were terrified when the storm arose which seemed likely to drown them, while He, on Whose protection they depended, slept, and appeared to have forgotten them. But our Lord had not forgotten them: it was His command that stilled the tempest, and He was as watchful to deliver them as to place them in danger. Why then should you be troubled by the trials your Saviour sends you? Why should you dislike the medicine which comes from the hands of your tender Father? God gives you those sufferings here, to save you from those of eternity. He says of His vineyard: 'I keep it night and day, there is no indignation in me against it' (Isaias xxvii, 3, 4). Trust in God's judgement, dear Sister, and not in your own, since He understands what is best for you, and knows the present and future state of your soul. Do not weary yourself to death with anxiety, for, as the Gospel says: 'You cannot with all your taking thought and caring add one cubit to your stature' (Matt. vi, 27). Close your eyes to all that affrights you and trust in the Wounds of Christ, Who received them for your sake, and you will find rest.

Remember that on the eve of their deliverance, God's chosen people were afflicted more than they had ever been; burden after burden was laid upon their shoulders and they were cruelly scourged. So it is that after a night of tempest the day dawns brightest, and when the travail is over, the mother rejoices in the birth of her child. You must believe that your trials are the heralds of great joy, for no soul deserves to possess peace and the delights of love until it has been wearied in combat and tasted the bitterness of spiritual desolation. Do not be disturbed if the time seems long in coming, for delay is not refusal especially when the promise has been given by Truth Himself. Your ears will surely one day hear the words: 'Arise, make haste my love, and come, for winter is now past, the rain is over and gone, the flowers are appearing'—flowers instead of thorns, and your soul shall cast away its mournfulness and bring forth the fruit of love.

*

IT is very plain, my dear sister, that you cannot bear being put to the test, nor have you yet emerged from spiritual childhood, for when your heavenly Bridegroom ceases to smile on you, you immediately imagine He is displeased with you. Where are the signal favours which you received from His blessed Hand as a pledge of His special love for you? Ought you so soon to forget how He has cherished you? or to believe that God would lightly withdraw affection He bestowed so fully? Why did He grant so many proofs of it, if not to make you trust Him? Be assured that He loves you, even if He does not show it at the present moment. You need not fear deception on this point, for, as I have often told you, our love for God should not cause us excessive sadness whenever we commit some venial sin. If this were necessary, who would ever be at rest or peace, for we are all sinners? May our Lord give you grace to lean on Him and rejoice in Him, placing your wounds in His, that you may be healed and comforted, however violent and painful your hurt may be.

How long will you continue your minute self-examinations? It is like raking up a dust heap from which nothing can come but rubbish and unpleasantness. Feel sure of this, that it is not for your own merits, but for those of Jesus crucified, that you are loved and made whole. Do not give way to such discouragement about your faults, the results will show you how displeasing it is to God. It would be far better to be courageous and strong-hearted. Meditate on the benefits you have received through Jesus Christ in the past and possess now; reflect on them in such a manner as to lead you to sorrow for your sins against Him and to avoid offending Him, without losing your peace and patience if you happen to fall. As I have often repeated, God loves you as you are. Be content that His love should come from His goodness, and not from your merits. What does it matter to a bride if she is not beautiful, if the bridegroom's affection for her makes her seem so in his eyes? If you look only on yourself, you will loathe yourself and your many defects will take away all your courage.

What more have you to wish for? In heaven there is One to Whom you appear all fair, for He looks at you through the apertures of the Wounds He received for you: by these He gives you grace, and supplies what is lacking in you, healing you and making you lovely. Be at peace: you are indeed the handmaid of the crucified Christ: forget your past misdoings as if they had never been. I tell you, in God's name, as I have done before, that such is His holy will. Run swiftly on your way with a light foot, like one who has thrown a heavy burden off his shoulders, which hindered his course. If the longed-for quiet does not come at once, do not distress yourself; sometimes one travels farther in a storm than in a calm, and war gains more merits than peace. He Who redeemed you will guide you aright so that you may be safe. Trust in Him; He has given you many reasons to do so; and when you consider your own defects, consider also the depths of His mercy which will help you far more than thinking about your deficiencies.

May God's mercy shelter you beneath His everlasting love, as I desire, and pray, and trust that it may, and for this I bid you hope. Recommend me to the same Lord for the sake of His love.

★

YOU ask me to give you some advice about saving your soul: a demand most reasonable and worthy to be granted if only my ability were equal to my good will.

When a man first has the use of his reason, he should begin so to regulate his life that when death comes his days may all have been spent in preparation for worthily receiving the crown of glory. When maturer age, the forerunner of death arrives, he must repent and make amends for any past negligence. This is the time to renew our courage and to exert ourselves to remedy the weaknesses of our youth and to devote ourselves with fervour to making ready for death.

This preparation consists not only in setting ourselves free from both debts and mortal sin, but in doing penance for our past faults, so that when our good and evil deeds are put into the balance of justice, with the divine mercy added to the right side of the scale, our attachment to God's service may weigh as much as our former attachment to the world. We ought to give alms, to be charitable, devout, patient and humble, in order to compensate for our former defects in these virtues. Busy like a honey-making bee, with a holy fervour, we should seek to get nearer and nearer to God; for at our time of life the hour approaches when we shall appear before Him. How shall we answer our Sovereign Judge, if we have spent carelessly those later years He has most mercifully given us, in which to amend the past and prepare ourselves for heaven?

Therefore, care less for temporal things and attend instead to those which are more important.

Withdraw your heart from the world before God takes your body from it: keep your mind in perfect peace however much it is occupied in business. A man who is travelling post haste concerning a matter which is of life and death to him, does not turn his head to look at anything as he passes. You must cultivate the same indifference to mundane matters. Say in your heart—'I am being led captive to death—what is this world to me? I am going to God; I do not wish to entangle myself in earthly things.' If in spite of all our efforts, we often find our attention distracted from religious matters, what would it be if we took no pains to be recollected? Consider that you are only beginning to serve God: remember your former good resolutions and beg God to assist you in carrying them out, for you have more experience as to the best means of keeping them now than you had before.

Your life consists in drawing nearer to God: to do this you must endeavour to detach yourself from visible things and remember that in a short time they will all be taken from you. Practise spiritual reading and prayer; go to confession and Holy Communion; and let the one object of your life be to serve God and to bear with things contrary to your will. Be most tender in your love for God and your neighbour; act in as charitable a way as possible to others, and be firm as a rock in bearing the trials sent you by Divine Providence. Good works are of no use unless we bear the cross as well, nor do sufferings profit us unless we lead a Christian life. If this seem hard to us, let us contemplate our Lord and Master, and see how many were His labours and pains. What He was, that He wishes His followers to be, each in his own measure, for He asked and obtained from His Father that where He was there might His servants also be. Therefore we must not fear to follow Him in His pains here below and yet wish to share with Him in His present bliss. Although it be the more painful part to partake of His sorrows, yet it is the better, for we shall enjoy our Lord's presence more fully for having toiled for Him here. 'If we suffer with Him, we shall also reign with Him.' Do not let us be incredulous about this promised reward nor slow in trying to gain it, for after a brief time of toil we shall enjoy eternal happiness.

Kindly consider this letter as written to your wife as well as to yourself. You must help each other and walk together in the right path so as to be companions in heaven mutually enjoying the sight of God, for He has 'joined you together on earth'.

DURING his early life John showed evidence of extraordinary piety. Born in the diocese of Toledo, his parents sent him at the age of fourteen to the University of Salamanca to study law. A year later he returned home with his father's consent as he found the subject uncongenial. A few years later he went to Alcalá to begin philosophy and theology under the guidance of the celebrated Dominican de Soto. On the death of his parents he intended to work in Mexico as a missionary. However, ecclesiastical authority induced him to renounce the idea in order to assist evangelism at home. All his life this secluded priest was a devoted lover of the Jesuits. He preached his first sermon in July, 1529. The life history of St. John of God was changed by the power of his preaching. For the remainder of his life Bl. John of Avila had bad health, and he died on 10th May, 1569. His tract *Audi Filia* and his *Spiritual Letters* were both translated into English in 1620 by L.T.

The second letter is addressed to 'a lady'.

Bl. Peter Faber

1506–1546

DEAREST Brother in Jesus Christ. May the grace and peace of our Redeemer be always in our souls. My excuse for not replying sooner to your letter is that I had no time to attend to it. There is no peace for me in the house. I could plead too that my hand is not so strong and steady as is necessary. But the best excuse of all is to say that I do not know whether what I have to offer you will meet your questions. However, I shall tell you some things which have now occurred to me. The first is, that whosoever desires to become useful to the heretics of this age must be solicitous to bear them much charity and to love them truly, excluding from his mind all thoughts which tend to cool his esteem for them. Secondly, it is necessary to gain their good will, so that they may love us to keep a place for us in their hearts. This we can achieve by familiar intercourse with them, speaking of the things we have in common and avoiding all contentious argument. . . . When we meet a man not only perverse in his opinions but evil in his life, we must go round about to persuade him to abandon his views before speaking to him of his errors in belief. It has happened to myself, for instance, that a man came wanting me to satisfy him about some erroneous views which he held, especially concerning the celibacy of the clergy. I dealt with him in such a way that he unburdened his conscience to me, on which lay the mortal sin of concubinage. I persuaded him to abandon that life . . . and no sooner had he done so and found himself by

God's grace able to live without a woman, than he also renounced his errors, without saying another word about them. . . . Some people have need of admonitions and exhortations on morals, on the fear and love of God, on good works, to counter their frailties, distractions, trepidities and other afflictions, which are not principally or in the first place from the understanding; but from the hands and feet of the body and soul.

★

I THINK no one was more grieved and troubled at my departure from Worms than the good Dean of St. Martin's, who had begun the Spiritual Exercises, and had scarcely finished the first week. He has, by God's grace, so profited by this that he is burning with zeal to soften the hearts of others, which are as hard as stones. There are many such in this city of Spires, to whom he has written about our concerns, and who, in consequence, have a great wish to make the Exercises. He has also written to the bishop here, who is one of the princes of Germany, and very well disposed. I have spoken to him several times, describing our manner of life, with which he is much edified. Last Thursday, he invited me to dine with him, when there were present the Duke of Bavaria and the Archbishop of Treves, and he afterwards sent to me his Vicar-General, whom, judging from our conversations on spiritual subjects, I consider very desirous of making the Exercises. I cannot, however, begin them, or undertake anything solid, as our departure for Ratisbon has just been fixed. However, as his lordship the bishop is to be there with the other German princes, it will be possible to take up the affair again, and to cultivate these good dispositions.

★

In the packet which I have from Cologne, I find a letter from Master Peter Canisius to me. I have read and read it again, and I cannot say whether it has given me more joy or sorrow of heart. For would not any one be moved to tears on hearing that you, who are so entirely one and the same in the union of your wills, are not allowed to dwell together in one house in that place; that you, who have shown so plainly that you have but one heart and soul, are thought unworthy to live in community? I could laugh for joy and weep for sorrow at the same time, when I think that these men insist on your living apart, and cannot endure you to be together; as if you would be better, separated in this way, than you were assembled in the same dwelling. I would fain say to these men who are disturbing and tormenting you, 'If you think the tree good, so also ought you to think the fruit; and if you think the tree evil, in like manner ought you to think the fruit evil.' But it is not prudent to tell the whole truth, especially in these troublous times. Our Lord be praised, Who gives you union in the spirit, though you are separated in the body. He will know how to gather together again the scattered remnant of Israel. Do you, on your part, place your whole trust in Him Who is the fountain of all grace.

*

DO not fear, my dearest father, that I shall ever forget you. Go on making ever more favourable to you that Divine Spirit, Who intercedes for you in the hearts of your friends. He watches over you with special care, and moves me to hold you in remembrance. I am also moved to do so by the benefits you have lavished on me and my brethren, and, above all, in obtaining for our Society a share in the good works of your order. That is reason enough for all

100

our brethren having a very special remembrance of you and your monastery. Last year I wrote to Master Francis Xavier, who is in India, begging him to make mention of you all in his prayers. At this time we are sending out thither ten of our Portuguese brethren, who are well acquainted with the favours we have received from you, and also with the love that I bear to your order, and to all Germany. They are conveying another letter from me to Master Francis, in which I have spoken of you and my other friends in Cologne, begging him further to acknowledge his share of our debt, and to help me with his prayers, that I may not be ungrateful to those who feel and act so kindly to me, beyond any desert of mine.

PETER FABER was a shepherd boy in Savoy who used to weep with longing for an education. By the autumn of 1529, when he first met Ignatius, the education was nearly achieved and Peter disillusioned. He held the highest place in his friend and master's estimation after St. Francis Xavier; and he was the first of the Jesuits to come to grips with the Protestant Reformation at Worms, Mainz, and Cologne. He was a man of very winning manners, great ability, and untiring energy. Exhausting work and constant travel were the cause of his death by fever in Rome in the arms of Ignatius, when about to leave for the Council of Trent. The *cultus* of Peter Faber was confirmed and ratified by Pope Pius IX in 1872.

St. Francis Xavier

1506–1552

MAY the grace and love of Christ our Lord also help and favour us! Amen.

Do not be surprised that I write to you so often. There are a great many here who are going to Portugal, and ask me for letters to take to you; and I am very glad to seize every opportunity of talking with you, and indeed I am so bold as to trust that what I feel so much fruit to my own soul in writing will not be read by you without pleasure, on account of the love that is between us.

The persons who will deliver to you this letter are two honourable and good men, excellent Christians, inhabitants of the city of Malacca, where they have their house and families. Their reason for their voyage is, that they have to discharge certain duties and obligations to which they were bound. They will tell you a great deal about the city of Malacca, about the labours of our Fathers there, and about the fruit which results from those labours. All these things they are perfectly well acquainted with, as being eye witnesses of all.

They take with them also letters from Father Francis Perez, in which I imagine he has done as he promised to do, that is, given a long, clear, and minute account of the results with which the functions proper to our Institute are there carried on. They will also tell you about the affairs of China and Japan, for they have been a long time at a place which lies so conveniently for traffic with those parts and countries that the people there know best of all what goes on in them. They say that all my friends and acquaintances wonder at me very much for trusting myself to so long and dangerous a voyage. I wonder much more at their little faith. Our Lord God has in His power the tempests of the Chinese and Japanese seas, which they say are as violent as any others anywhere in the whole world. To His power all the winds are subject, all the rocks and the whirlpools and the quicksands and shoals, which they say are to be found in those seas in such great numbers, so dangerous, so sadly famous for the shipwrecks they have caused. He also holds in His sway all the pirates of whose numberless hordes they tell us, and who are exceedingly savage and are wont to put to death with exquisite tortures all whom they take prisoners, and especially all Portuguese. And as this our Lord God has all these things under His dominion, I fear nothing from any of them. I only fear God Himself, lest He should decree some just chastisement upon me on account of my negligence in His service, and because I am by fault of my own unfit and useless for the work of advancing the Kingdom and Name of His Son Jesus Christ among the nations who know them not. Except this, I fear nothing, and I count as naught all those other causes of fear, dangers, labours, and the like, which my timid friends vie with one another in pressing upon me as so very formidable. I laugh at them all in full security, and the simple fear of God alone extinguishes in me all fear of His creatures; for I know that they can hurt no one, except those to whom and as far as their Creator allows them to be causes of trouble.

But to return to our two friends. I pray you for all the regard you have for the love and service of our Lord God, that for the few days during which they are to be at Lisbon you take care of them tenderly, see that they are provided with a convenient lodging, and help them in all things according to your ability and their requirements. And when you have heard all the many things that they will have to tell you about India, and you send them back with their business all finished, then be careful to give them long and accurate letters to carry to us, informing us all about all the fathers and brothers of our Society who are in Italy, France, the Low Countries, Germany, Castile, and Aragon, and in particular about that blessed College of Coimbra which is so dear to me. These letters you should direct, I think, to our Fathers at Malacca. The original will be given to them by these two citizens of Malacca on their return home, and will be kept there, and copies of them will be sent to us from the port of Malacca—whence many ships sail yearly for China and Japan—by such a number of ways, that they will reach us by some one of them at least which will escape all accidents. May our Lord God bring us together in His holy glory in Paradise! Amen.

Your most devoted and loving brother in Christ,

FRANCIS

The other letter of introduction shows us a little more of the manner in which Francis was always trying to lead those who applied to him for any favour to look after the concerns of their soul as well as their temporal interests. It also gives the first hint of what afterwards exercised an important influence on his schemes and movements—an increased vigilance and severity on the part of the Chinese government as to the exclusion of foreigners, especially Portuguese, from their ports.

*

MAY the grace and love of Christ our Lord always help and favour us! Amen.

The person who will deliver this letter to you is a man

with whom I have a certain amount of acquaintance. He is going to Portugal in order to ask the King for a reward for some service which he has done to the state, and has urgently pressed me to give him letters of recommendation to you as to that business. Now I am quite aware, and I have not concealed from my friend himself, that it would be much more profitable to employ himself in another branch of the art of petitioning—applying, that is, to God, and obtaining from Him the pardon of his sins— than to go supplicating from a mortal king an earthly reward for his merits and good deeds. But it was not possible to persuade him, at least here, to give up his hopes and intentions. I am of opinion that when he lands in Portugal you should try whether the change of scene has changed his mind in this respect; and if perchance the evils and dangers of the voyage have made him more amenable to heavenly admonitions, then persuade him rather to stay in Portugal as a monk than to come out here again as a soldier. If you succeed, you will have done the poor wretch a very great kindness, and have made gain of a soul that was lost. But if his mind be still fixed on transitory things, and he be not able to rise to such a height of philosophy as I mention, then by all means let him have your help in obtaining his just demands, and use your influence, as far as you may, that out of the rewards which he has earned by long service as a soldier he may have at least so much given him as may be enough for him to live on at home. And I beg you again and again, for the love of God, to attempt to get this done for His sake.

After I had written all the letters which I had determined to send to Portugal by the hand of Pedro Fernandez, who has discharged in these countries of India the office of Vicar to the Bishop, some ships arrived here from Malacca, bringing certain news that the Chinese ports are unfavourable and hostile to the Portuguese. This, however, will not frighten me from attempting the voyage to Japan, which I mean by the help of God to undertake, as I have already told you that I have made up my mind to do. There is nothing more fruitful of good to the soul in this life of misery than to live in the midst of great dangers of death, the true and only cause for braving which has been the simple love of God and of pleasing Him, and the sincere desire to extend our holy religion. Believe me, it is sweeter for a man to live in labours of this sort, than to pass his time in peace and leisure without them. May our Lord God unite us in His holy glory! Amen.

Your most loving brother in Christ,
FRANCIS

★

I BEG you most earnestly and desire of you that, for the love which you bear to Jesus Christ, and for the desire which you have for the glory of God, you make it your study everywhere to be 'a good saviour' of Christ, and set yourself as an example of all virtues to the city in which you are, and avoid altogether giving any offence to the people. You will succeed in what I say, if moderation and Christian humility shine out in all you do. So at the beginning you must exercise yourself diligently in humble and abject offices, and then the people of the town will be won to you in this manner, and will take whatever you do in good part; much more, of course, if they see that you persevere in the cause with daily increased ardour. Wherefore I earnestly pray you not to forget your own progress in virtue: for you are well aware that one who does not make progress in virtue, goes backwards.

I again, then, ask of you and beg of you for the sake of God, let your example excite the people to piety. If you are well furnished with humility of mind and with prudence, I do not doubt that you will both reap good results from your labours and become a really good preacher. Humility and prudence are the parents and teachers of many great deeds. You must visit very often the hospitals and the prisons. These offices of Christian humility, besides that they are pleasing to God and helpful to men, have also the effect of making people esteem highly those who practise them and respect them much, even though they have not the office of preachers nor any facility of preaching.

You must diligently gain to yourself and keep as diligently the love of the Commandant, the Vicar, the clergy, the Brethren of Mercy, the King's magistrates, and indeed the whole city. This general regard is of great moment to enable missioners to turn in the right direction the wills of men, both by preaching and by hearing confessions, and paying visits. It is my great desire that in your work of cherishing and increasing this new Christian community, you should be aided by the authority and assistance of the Commandant, the Vicar, and the Brethren of the Confraternity of Mercy. Take pains, therefore, that whatever increase may accrue to the worship of God by means of you be all attributed to their exertions. Thus it will be that they will give more help to your endeavours, and hinder them less. You will also gain another thing—that in your difficulties and contentions you will have many more friends and protectors, and fewer adversaries, or rather none at all. For who will venture to attack you, when you are known to be covered by the protection of men of such position? So if at any time you are writing to the King of Portugal about the propagation of the faith, you must make honourable and grateful mention of their remarkable zeal for Christian interests, and if you think well you may show them your letters, and by all means ask the King to let them know that their good offices towards us and towards religion have been very pleasing to his Highness, and to speak in the letters in approbation of their zeal in such a way, as to attribute to them chiefly, after God, all the increase that has been made in the divine worship and the Christian religion.

You must never write to the King except about matters relating to religion, and to the conversion of the heathen. As to all other matters, you ought to write to the Society in Portugal. In order to avoid giving offence to people, I should wish you not to collect the revenues of the College and of the new converts, either in person or through any other of the Society, if this can be avoided, but rather by means of some pious man fit for the commission. For I do not suppose it would be difficult to find some wealthy person to act as agent, so that he may neither manage the business at any risk to our income, nor be too vexatious in his exaction from the poor. Such a man you should instruct in meditation on divine truths, then lead him on to frequent the sacraments, and then, with his own good-will and desire, set him over the business of which I speak. May God in His goodness unite us in Heaven!

★

MAY the grace and love of Jesus Christ our Lord be ever with us to help and favour us! Amen.

A namesake of yours, Melchior Gonzalez, has given me your letter, which I have read with no small pleasure. May God give you the grace to scatter a 'good odour' on the Society where you are, now that there is so much feeling of offence against us among the people there. I pray and conjure you with all the earnestness I can, by all the desire which you have to serve and please God our Lord, take the most efficacious means in your power to conciliate people to yourself and to the Society, and to leave nothing undone, however difficult, that comes in your way to do to this end. If you are humble and prudent, I am in great hopes that by God's help you will gain great fruit there. I send to you from this Francesco Enriquez, that he may stay at Tana with Manuel. Osorio may remain with you for household duties, and Barreto to teach reading and writing; you yourself, meanwhile, being occupied in spiritual ministrations, and in conversing piously and holily with men of all sorts, as well as in explaining the Christian doctrine and in preaching.

As for your sermons, I have been very much pleased with what you write to me as to your system of preparation, as to the form and whole method which you have determined to follow in them. I think you should keep to this method, and practise yourself in the manner you suggest as often as possible, for I hope in good confidence that the favour of God will not be wanting to you, that if you are humble you will turn out a great preacher. Send Francesco Lopez to this College by the first ship which sails hitherwards from you. Take care often to read over the written instructions I have given you as to the way of carrying on the advancement of the Gospel where you are. You will learn many other things from your own practice and the experience of events, if you are humble and prudent, if you carefully watch what occurs, considering and comparing all with the advice and orders which you have received from hence. Francesco Enriquez is to live at Tana, whither he is now sent, under your authority. I should wish you to give him an order of obedience most diligently to avoid giving offence to any one, and to show himself meek and signally patient on all occasions. You must also inquire from others, by means of watchers whom you can trust, whether he or anyone else of ours give to anybody a just cause of offence. If you find that it is so, meet the matter at once without delay, applying some fitting remedy to the evil. Thus is is that I would have you watch first over yourself, and then over others. But if you should find anyone of ours guilty of a serious sin which goes so far as to give public scandal, and to irritate the people against us not altogether without reason, then at once dismiss him from the Society; for I now from this moment consider as dismissed those whom you may dismiss. For I have so much confidence in your prudence, that I am certain that no one will be sent away by you except for just cause.

As to the annual income of your College, take care that it is spent rather in the building up of spiritual temples than of those which are sensible and material. Of this second class of sacred buildings, which have to be raised up of wood or stone, you must spend money upon none, except such as are absolutely necessary, such as you cannot refuse to build without the very gravest public inconvenience. If any plans of building are set before you with no other recommendation than that they will improve the splendour of decoration or present a more stately outside, decline them on the ground that it is requisite to postpone them to more urgent calls, and they can well be put off to more convenient times. Whatever you may have over and above from your income, spend, as I told you, in educating native boys in wholesome knowledge and good manners. For these are spiritual temples in which God is better honoured than in others, since when these boys have grown up to be men, they will by means of their good example, and by spreading the teaching which has been given them, be instruments for God of matters which most greatly concern His glory and the salvation of men.

A few days ago I sent you from hence Paul of Guzerat, who has been a pupil of this College for many years. He is a good speaker in the language of the people, and is sufficiently furnished with learning to teach the elements of the faith to the Christian natives. He would also be able to preach usefully to the people, if some of ours who are not so ready as he is in the vernacular would supply, as occasion requires, his lack of fuller erudition, by putting his arguments in proper shape and giving him matter for his sermons.

I quite approve of what you say in your letter about the revenue of the College, that you think we should faithfully take care that it be spent according to the intention of the King, as signified in the document of its foundation. That is just what I also wish by all means to be done, both because it is an obligation of justice to do so, and in order that the people may not be scandalized, seeing—which God forbid—that this is neglected. But after you have abundantly provided for the needs of all the poor who are at Bazain, according to the prescription of the royal diploma, then, if there is any surplus, there can be no doubt that it would be rightly spent, and spent not against the King's will, in contributing to the aid of the poor boys we have here, especially those who are natives of Bazain, and those who may hereafter be useful there, as we see in the instance of this Paul of Guzerat. So if out of the collection of clothes which is usually distributed every year from the funds of your College to the poor at Bazain you have any bundles of stuff which are not wanted by the people there, you may send them to us, if at least this can be done without any complaint or offence on the part of anyone. For we have here a seminary full of lads, for whose clothing the arrival of such a present would be very convenient— on the condition, however, as I said, that nothing at all be taken away from any of the poor at Bazain, who have the first right to the benefit of this bounty of his Highness. You must see, therefore, that the wants and desires of all these are faithfully satisfied, in order that our consciences may be free from burthen and for the greater service of God. If, when this obligation has been fulfilled, no crumbs remain for you to scatter in this direction, then we will make up our minds to bear contentedly the absence of such aid.

For the rest, apply yourself entirely to the exercise of preaching and of hearing confessions, visiting and consoling the sick in the hospital, and the prisoners in the gaol, and in other like works of charity to your neighbour, being always ready to run to all duties of the kind as often as you are invited to them by the managers of the Confraternity of Mercy, whose special business they are. If you practise such ministrations with charity and humility, the result will be, by the good gift of God, that you will have favour and authority with the citizens, and however little natural eloquence you may possess, yet that little which you are able to bring to bear will do much, because it will be strengthened by the companionship of zeal and modesty, and by means of it you will produce a great movement among the minds of the people, and gather in very rich fruits. Only take care—and this I press upon your attention again and again—take care to keep up the closest union and friendship with the Bishop's Vicar and the other priests in the place, with the Commandant, the magistrates, and the King's officials, and conduct yourself prudently, kindly, humbly, and with thorough goodwill towards the whole population. Believe me, the best hope of success in preaching is not to be placed in exquisite learning, or elegant diction, or in display, or in a sort of scenic exhibition of eloquence. The head and sum of the art lies in being approved of by those whom you address, and in pleasing them, and in gaining the keys of their hearts before you knock at the doors of their ears. If your audience love you, you will persuade them to do whatever you will, and you will easily win a great many souls to God if you never alienate any one from yourself.

Next September, at which time I hope to be at Malacca, let me find full and copious letters to meet me there from you, informing me distinctly and minutely of the fruit of your ministrations. You should write also to the fathers of this College, and of course much oftener, on account of your near neighbourhood and of the multitude of persons who pass from the one place to the other. May our Lord God bring us together in the glory of Paradise! Amen.

Your brother in Christ,
FRANCIS

*

TWICE in the day you will recollect yourself—in the morning as soon as you awake, and in the evening, and for the space of an hour and a half, or an hour at the least, you will meditate on the life of Christ our Saviour, following the method prescribed in the book of the *Spiritual Exercises* of our holy Father Ignatius, with regard to the division of the mysteries, as well as for all the rest; and at the end of your meditation, both morning and evening, renew your vows of poverty, chastity, and obedience; for this is the perpetual sacrifice offered in the living temples of religious souls—the sacrifice most acceptable to God, and by means of which they acquire most strength and gain most grace for repelling the assaults of the enemy. Before you retire to rest for the night, never fail to examine your conscience, repassing your thoughts, words, and actions of the day, noticing the offences you have committed against God as minutely as if you were going to confess them: then beg pardon of the divine majesty, purpose amendment, and recite a *Pater Noster* and an *Ave Maria*. For a moment or two consider how you may best correct yourself. On awaking in the morning, let it be your first care to recall to mind the defects noticed in your examen the previous night, humbling yourself and deploring them. Whilst dressing yourself, prepare for meditation, and at the same time beg grace of Almighty God not to fall into any new faults in the course of the present day; for this is about the best disposition you can carry with you to meditation. Make it a point of conscience not to neglect any part of these exercises, nor even to change the order of them; and if you fail (unless it be from infirmity or other lawful hindrance) let not the day pass without acknowledging your fault and doing penance for it. Let it be your chief care to overcome yourself, always contradicting your own inclination, enduring and embracing what you most dislike and abhor: study in all things to be depressed and humbled, because without true humility you will never become spiritual, nor be useful to the salvation of your neighbour, nor be caressed by the saints, nor be pleasing to God, nor persevere in this our little Society, which could never tolerate proud, arrogant men—men addicted to their own judgement or tenacious of their own honour: for, indeed, such sort of people never conform themselves to anything. Do you, on the contrary, obey every superior in whatever he may command, without contradiction or excuse, but with the same exactitude and promptitude as you would obey our holy Father Ignatius himself. In like manner, give him a full account of your soul, disclosing to him separately and singly your temptations, your evil inclinations of character, etc.; because, besides this being necessary to enable him to apply the necessary remedies, the very act of humiliation undergone in making these disclosures, subjecting oneself to another, (how much more when he is a superior!) is of itself often sufficient to put the devil to flight; for, as he often does more by deceit than by open force, to discover him is to overthrow him. Moreover, the most sure and expeditious means to obtain the light and grace of God is to seek it from those who hold his place in our regard.

FRANCIS was born in Castle Xavier and was the youngest of a large family. Xavier was one of the first to join the Society of Jesus which Ignatius had founded, and was ordained priest in 1537. In 1541, to his great joy, he was chosen to go to the East Indies. He set out with nothing but his Bible, Breviary, and crucifix. The ship in which he sailed was crowded with soldiers. He ate the scraps left from their table, and found a bed on some coil of ropes. He tended the sick and diseased. At Mozambique he nearly lost his life from a fever caught in ministering to others. On recovery he proceeded to Goa, nominally a Christian town. He was heart-stricken at the depravity of the people. He at once set to work to bring about some reform. After some years' successful work in Goa the call came for him to go to the poor pearl fishermen of Cape Comorin. He lived and worked among them for many months, eating their poor fare of rice, teaching them at first by signs only. Some years later he went to Travancore. His preaching met with a wonderful response. He is said to have baptized 10,000 in one month. He next crossed to Malacca, the great centre of traffic between India and China and Japan.

In 1548 Xavier left for Japan with a young Japanese convert to carry on his missionary work in that country. Many converts were made, and when he returned to Malacca in 1552 he left many others behind to carry on his work. He reached the island Sancin, where he was stricken down with a fever. Antonio, a Chinese lad, was his only attendant. He lay in an old wood hut on the beach. After three days of severe suffering the soul of this great apostle of the heathen entered into rest, with the last words of the *Te Deum* on his lips, 'O Lord, in Thee have I trusted; let me never be confounded'.

He died on 2nd December, 1552, aged 46. His body was first buried on that lonely shore, but afterwards translated to Goa, where his relics still remain.

This man of the Basque nobility was one to whom nothing mattered at all save the Gospel. He went to the Orient and baptized tens of thousands, and India beheld in him its first great Christian propagandist. Later he wrestled in spirit with the *bonzes* of Japan and even dreamed of the spiritual conquest of China.

The first two letters are letters of introduction addressed to Simon Rodriguez in 1549. The third and the fourth were written in 1552 to Father Melchior Nuñez. The last letter consists of rules of conduct.

St. Francis Borgia

1510–1572

OUR Lord knows how anxiously I have hoped
that your Majesty would, in compliance with the general
expectation, pay a visit to Italy on your way home. I am
certain that in this case your Majesty would have been
graciously pleased to grant me an audience, in order that I
might say by word of mouth all that I am now doing
myself the honour of putting on paper. But in whatever
manner I offer myself to your notice, I can only do so with
a sense of extreme confusion, being, as your Majesty must
be only too well aware, a miserable sinner, and having
been far from giving the edification I ought, during the
period of my sojourn at the Imperial Court. For this I
crave your forgiveness, and I am ready to make any
satisfaction which it may seem fit either to my earthly
Sovereign or to my Heavenly King to impose upon me.
I trust that you will extend towards me your royal clem-
ency, remembering how Almighty God has preserved me
alive until the present day, although I have over and over
again deserved to be cast down into the very depths of
Hell, on account of my innumerable transgressions. He
has, moreover, opened the eyes of my soul, and enabled me
to see what He has done for me, and what I have done
against Him.

Immediately after the death of the Duchess of Gandia,
He inspired me with the resolution at which I have finally
arrived after a lengthened period of mature deliberation,
and after due consultation with many servants of God, who

have not ceased to offer for me their prayers and the Holy Sacrifice of the Mass. My wish to give myself altogether to Him has increased day by day, as His grace has gradually dispelled the darkness of my heart, until at last I have ventured to enter the vineyard of the Lord and offer to work there, although as yet I have spent my life in doing nothing but harm. It has pleased His infinite goodness, which is like an ocean without bottom or shore, so to influence His servants who belong to the Society of Jesus, that they have admitted me into their Order. As yet I have been unable to carry out my design of leaving the world in order to serve God as a Jesuit *usque ad mortem*, because I have been obliged to discharge the duties of a father in regard to my children. I hope, however, in the course of two or three months at the furthest, to find myself altogether free, and I believe that the Fathers of the Society will then allow me to take up my permanent abode in their midst. Under these circumstances I have no alternative except to implore your Majesty, as your humble servant and subject, and as Commander of your Majesty's Order of St. James, to give me the greatest possible proof of the favour with which you have ever been graciously pleased to regard me. I beseech you to give me leave to spend the remainder of my days in lamenting over my past sins, and striving to make atonement for them, in recognizing the full extent of the miseries and dangers which surround me in the present, and in providing against the uncertainties of the future. Should our Lord vouchsafe me grace sufficient to correct my evil life and become more acceptable in His sight, I promise to offer my prayers and Holy Sacrifices without ceasing, for the temporal welfare of your Majesty, and still more for your eternal salvation. May God, Who has enabled your Majesty to win such signal victories over heretics and unbelievers, enable you to conquer no less completely the enemies of your soul and your own sinful inclinations, so that you may say with the Apostle: 'God forbid that I should glory, save in the Cross of our Lord Jesus Christ.' Those who have not altogether lost their taste for spiritual things, can find true happiness nowhere but in this Cross. All the pleasures of the world seem to them heavy and wearisome, when once they have experienced the sweetness of the Saviour's yoke, so that it seems to them a grievous thing if they have no cross to carry, and are left to live on without trials or sufferings. I beg Him Who endured so much upon the Cross for your Majesty's sake, to be pleased to guard and watch over your Imperial person.

FRANCIS was the son of the Duke of Gandia, in Spain. After many appointments in the royal court he was made governor of Catalonia. Succeeding to the dukedom on the death of his father in 1543, he fortified Gandia against the Moors, and founded a college of Jesuits in that town. His wife died in 1546 and, after seeing his children of age and settled in life, Francis joined the Society of Jesus in 1551. He was ordained priest, and preached throughout both Spain and Portugal. St. Ignatius made him Vicar-General for Spain and he became the third General of the Order in 1565. St. Francis died in 1572 and his relics are in the Jesuit church in Madrid.

The above letter was written from Rome in 1551 and was addressed to the Emperor Charles V who was then residing at Augsburg.

Bl. William Hart

Died 1583

MOST dear and loving Mother,
Seeing that by the severity of the laws, by the wickedness of our times, and by God's holy ordinance and appointment, my days in this life are cut off, of duty and conscience I am bound (being far from you in body, but in spirit very near you) not only to crave your daily blessing, but also to write these few words unto you.

You have been a most loving, natural, and careful mother unto me; you have suffered great pains in my birth and bringing up; you have toiled and turmoiled to feed and sustain me, your first and eldest child; and, therefore, for these, and all other your motherly cherishings, I give you (as it becometh me to do) most humble and hearty thanks, wishing that it lay in me to show myself as loving, natural and dutiful a son as you have showed yourself a most tender and careful mother. But I cannot express my love, show my duty, declare my affection, testify my good will towards you; so little I am able to do, so much I think myself bound unto you.

I had meant this spring to have seen you if God had granted me health and liberty; but now never shall I see you, or any of yours, in this life again; trusting yet in heaven to meet you, to see you, to live everlastingly with you.

Alas! Sweet mother, why do you weep? Why do you lament? Why do you take so heavily my honourable death? Know you not that we are born once to die, and that always in this life we may not live? Know you not how vain, how wicked, how inconstant, how miserable this life of ours is? Do you not consider my calling, my estate, my profession? Do you not remember that I am going to a place of all pleasure and felicity? Why then do you weep? Why do you mourn? Why do you cry out?

But perhaps you will say, I weep not so much for your death as I do for that you are hanged, drawn, and quartered. My sweet mother, it is the favourablest, honourablest, and happiest death that ever could have chanced unto me. I die not for knavery, but for verity; I die not for treason, but for religion; I die not for any ill demeanour or offence committed, but only for my Faith, for my conscience, for my priesthood, for my blessed Saviour Jesus Christ; and, to tell you truth, if I had ten thousand lives, I am bound to lose them all rather than to break my faith, to lose my soul, to offend my God.

We are not made to eat, drink, sleep, to go bravely, to feed daintily, to live in this wretched vale continually; but to serve God, to please God, to fear God, to keep His commandments; which when we cannot be suffered to do, then rather must we choose to lose our lives than to desire our lives.

Neither am I alone in this kind of suffering, for there have of late suffered twenty or twenty-two priests, just, virtuous, and learned men, for the self-same cause for which I do now suffer. You see Mr. James Fenn and John Body are imprisoned for religion, and I dare say they are desirous to die the same death which I shall die. Be contented, therefore, good mother; stay your weeping, and comfort yourself that you have borne a son that hath lost his life and liberty for God Almighty's sake, Who shed His most precious blood for him. If I did desire to look for preferment or promotion, credit or estimation in this world, I could do as others do; but alas! I pass not for this trish-trash; I contemn this wretched world; I detest the pleasures and commodities thereof, and only desire to be in heaven with God, where I trust I shall be before this my last letter come to you.

Be of good cheer, then, my most loving mother, and cease from weeping, for there is no cause why you should do so. Tell me, for God's sake, would you not be glad to see me a bishop, a king, or an emperor? Yes, verily, I dare say you would. How glad, then, may you be to see me a martyr, a saint, a most glorious and bright star in heaven. The joy of this life is nothing, and the joy of after life is everlasting; and therefore thrice happy may you think yourself that your son William is gone from earth to heaven, and from a place of all misery to a place of all felicity.

I wish that I were near to comfort you, but because that cannot be, I beseech you, even for Christ Jesus' sake, to comfort yourself. You see how God hath brought me up, and how He hath blessed me many ways; a thousand times, then, unhappy should I be if for His sake I should not lose this miserable life to gain that blessed and eternal life wherein He is.

I can say no more, but desire you to be of good cheer, because myself am well. If I had lived, I would have helped you in your age, as you have helped me in my youth. But now I must desire God to help you and my brethren, for I cannot. Good mother, be contented with that which God hath appointed for my perpetual comfort; and now, in your old days, serve God after the old Catholic manner. Pray unto Him daily; beseech Him heartily to make you a member of His Church, and that He will save your soul. For Jesus' sake, good mother, serve God. Read that Book that I gave you, and die a member of Christ's body, and then one day we shall meet in heaven, by God's grace.

Recommend me to my father-in-law, to my brethren, to Andrew Gibbon's mother, and to Mrs. Body, and all the rest. Serve God, and you cannot do amiss. God comfort you. Jesus save your soul, and send you to heaven. Farewell, good mother, farewell ten thousand times. Out of York Castle, the tenth of March, 1583.

Your most loving and obedient son,
WILLIAM HART

FEW writings display the spirit of Christian courage as strongly as the above letter, written from his dungeon in York Castle to his mother by Blessed William Hart. A native of Wells in Somerset, he left Lincoln College, Oxford, for the sake of his Catholic belief, and went to Douai, Rheims, and Rome, where he was ordained priest before returning to England. The field of his labours was Yorkshire.

His charity was very remarkable towards a number of Catholics that were prisoners for their conscience. These he daily visited, refusing no labour nor danger for their comfort and assistance, encouraging them to suffer with patience, procuring them what assistance he was able, hearing their confessions, and administering the sacraments to them. Once he had to escape by letting himself down over the castle wall into the moat, where he was up to the chin in mud and water. He was betrayed by an apostate, arrested on Christmas night and hanged on 15th March, 1583.

St. Teresa of Avila

1515–1582

MAY the grace of the Holy Ghost be ever with your Paternity. Last week I wrote to you at great length on the same subject on which I now write, and sent this to you by two different routes, so anxious was I that one at least of these letters should reach you. Yesterday two letters from your Paternity were handed to me . . . the date of them was not so recent as I should have wished, nevertheless I was much consoled to learn by them that you were in good health. May our Saviour keep you in it. All your daughters ask this of Him. It is the almost continual prayer of these monasteries which are also yours. Our sisters know no other father than you, and all bear you the same affection. This is not surprising, because we have no greater good on earth than to be under obedience to you; and as all are well pleased, they are never tired of expressing the gratitude they owe you for having helped the Reform in its first beginnings. . . . Please God that the differences between you and the discalced may be softened, and that they may no longer be a cause of trouble to you. Though they are able to justify their conduct and I know them to be true sons to your Paternity, submissive, and anxious not to give you displeasure, yet on several points I consider they were to blame. . . . There have been great disputes, especially between Fr. Mariano and me, for he is very high-spirited. As for Fr. Gratian, he has behaved like an angel. If he had been alone matters would have turned out differently.

Oh, my dear and venerated father, you cannot see what goes on here. But I see it, and I tell you because I know your holiness and love of virtue. The friars of the Observance say one thing to your Paternity, another here. They tell you they cannot understand how you can treat virtuous men in such way. They go to the archbishop and make out that they are innocent of all designs against our monasteries, and then they have recourse to you. . . . As for me, reverend father, I see both one and the other, and God knows I am speaking the truth. I think your sons of the discalced Order are those who are the most faithful to you, and will always be so. . . . The sole wish of the friars is to be assisted by you as your sons, and it is one that reason demands you should accord them. To do otherwise would be to displease God. Let your Paternity recommend the matter to our Divine Master. Forget the past, as a true father should. Remember that you are a servant of the Blessed Virgin, and that she would be displeased if you abandoned her sons who are working for the increase of her Order at the price of their utmost endeavours.

*

UNLESS I were obliged, my lord, under obedience, I should not answer; and for good reasons I should refuse to judge the subject under discussion. Not, however, as our sisters here will have it, because my brother being one of the rival competitors my affection for him would give reason to suspect my impartiality. No! for all the competitors are dear to me, having all helped me in my labours. Moreover, my brother was the last comer, who only appeared as we finished drinking the chalice; but he also shared it; and he shall have an even better share later, by the grace of God. May God grant too that I say nothing which may cause me to be denounced to the Inquisition; for my head is tired out with the number of letters, and other things, which I have had to write since last night. But as obedience can do everything with me, I am going to comply, well or ill, with your lordship's orders. I should have liked to have taken a little time to read over and enjoy the papers; but you are not satisfied with my doing this, and I must obey.

First of all, it appears that the words in question come from the Spouse of our souls, Who says to them, 'Seek thyself in Me.' I do not require more to conclude that Don Francisco is beside the question when he says that it signifies God is present in everything. Truly a grand discovery! But here is something more, and unless Don Francisco does not contradict it I shall have to denounce him to my neighbour the Inquisition. He is ever saying and repeating in his paper, 'St. Paul says this', or 'the Holy Ghost expresses Himself in this way': and after that he says —by way of conclusion—that his essay is full of follies. He will certainly have to retract as quickly as he can, or he will see what will happen!

As for Fr. Julian, he begins well but ends badly; thus he will certainly not get the prize. He is not asked here to explain how the uncreated and created light became united; nor what a soul feels who is perfectly united to her Creator; nor whether in this state she differs or not from her divine Objective, etc. Again, what does he mean by the expression, *when the soul is purified*? As for me, I believe virtues and purification of the soul are insufficient here, because it is a question of a supernatural state, and a gift which God confers on whomsoever He pleases; and if anything could predispose the soul to receive it, it would be love. But I forgive him his digressions, because he has at least one merit: he is less lengthy than my Fr. John of the Cross.

The doctrine of the last named would be excellent for one who wished to make the Exercises of St. Ignatius; here they are out of place. We should be much to be pitied if we could not seek God before being dead to the world. What! were the Magdalen, the Samaritan woman, the Canaanitess, already dead to the world when they found their Saviour? He enlarges greatly on the necessity of uniting one's self with God in order to be made one—wholly—with Him. But when that happens, when the soul has received this signal favour from God, He can no longer tell her to seek Him, for she has already found Him. The Lord preserve me from people who are so spiritual that they wish, without choice or examination, to bring all back to a perfect state of contemplation. We must, withal, do him the justice of acknowledging that he has explained remarkably well what we never asked to know. This comes of discussing such a subject: the profit one reaps from it is the one we least expected to get.

This is precisely what has happened to Don Lorenzo de Cepeda. We are much obliged to him for his answer and his verses. He was speaking somewhat out of his depth. But in consideration of the little treat he has given us, we willingly forgive his want of humility in treating upon subjects which, as he himself acknowledges, were so much above him. He would deserve, however, to be expostulated with for the good advice he gives to devout souls—without their having asked for it—to practise the prayer of quiet, as if it depended on them; God grant that he may get some good of his intercourse with such spiritual-minded people. Still his work did not fail to please me, though I think he has great reason to be ashamed of it.

In short, my lord, it is impossible to decide which of these writings is the best, as one cannot say, in justice, that any are faultless. Will you please to tell their authors to correct themselves; and perhaps I should not do amiss to correct myself too, so that I may not resemble my brother in being wanting in humility? I conclude, my lord, for fear of fatiguing you with my extravagances. I will answer at another time the letter you do me the honour of writing to me, for which I thank you heartily.

*

JESUS! May the grace of the Holy Spirit ever be with you. Amen.

I assure you that this is a real mortification to me! Do you fancy that I am too far off to know what you are doing and to feel it keenly? No, indeed, it rather grieves me the more for I know what a consolation your favour is to the sisters and what a help it is to them to have you for their confessor. The Mother Prioress told me this and that she is much pained by your decision, and with good reason.

Though the Father Provincial is there and hears the nuns' confessions, they will not all care to keep to one confessor, nor need your courtesy lead you to retire. I regret I was not there at the time you were confessor; and I trust you will pray for me. I am quite satisfied with any priest who is a discalced Carmelite when the Father Provincial approves of him as chaplain: how much more am I contented with one who possesses your qualities!

I do not write more often because we have news of one another from the Mother Prioress, and I am so busy here that my life there was one of rest in comparison with this. But I never forget your Honour in my poor prayers and beg you to remember me in yours.

The unworthy servant of your Honour,
TERESA DE JESUS

*

JESUS! May the grace of the Holy Spirit ever be with you. Amen.

I must tell you that yesterday the Bishop sent us twelve bushels of wheat. As the alms was given in your name, it is well for you to know of it in case you should meet his Lordship. Please let me know how this wet season agrees with your health and whether you have been to confession for the feast of this glorious Saint, for he is a very great Saint and one for whom you ought to feel a special devotion because of your love for the poor.

Doña Maria tells me that she will not acquit you of your debt for the reliquary until you give it to me. She speaks as though it belonged to her, but it seems to me that you too had a right to it. As it is God Himself Who will repay this kindness as well as the rest you show us, He will understand the question and decide justly. May His Majesty have you in His keeping and guidance for many a year. The Mother Prioress and nuns here beg you to remember them in your prayers.

The unworthy servant of your Honour,

TERESA DE JESUS

*

JESUS be with your Reverence.

I am very sorry to withdraw the two sisters from your convent, but it cannot be helped, though, as the one who gave you trouble is going, you must be patient and pray that they may fulfil their duty well so as not to destroy the good reputation of your house. I hope this will be the case, for I am leaving some excellent nuns with them.

It seems to me that you have not completely recovered from your illness. It is a great mercy from God that you are able to move about again. For love of Him, take care of yourself. God grant that you may leave your present house, for I assure you I feel very anxious about you. His Majesty must wish you to suffer in every way. May He be praised for all, and may He repay you for the lemons. I was feeling so ill the day before that I was glad to have them, and the veils as well, for I was wearing a threadbare one inside out and those you send me are very good. Be kind enough to give me nothing more until I ask for it, but spend the money in getting nourishing food for yourself instead.

We are so well off in this foundation that I do not know how it will succeed. Will you all ask our Lord to give us a good house, for we have changed our mind about taking the hermitage. There are many good and suitable places: a number of people are looking after the matter, and the Bishop never ceases showing us kindness. Be good enough to pray for him and those who are helping us.

Will you write a note to Fray Domingo (Bañez), if I am unable, telling him about this foundation. I shall try to do so, but if I cannot, remember me very kindly to him.

I was delighted at your having provided for the two sisters from Salamanca so completely: it is not everyone who does so, though it was quite right, especially as regards Mother Isabel de Jesus, to whom you owe it: she seems very happy. As she and the rest will tell you all the news, and I have other letters to write, I will say no more except that I beg our Lord to have you in His keeping and to grant you all the sanctity I ask of Him. Amen.

The Missals you sent are so handsome that I do not know when we shall be able to repay you for them.

The servant of your Reverence,

TERESA DE JESUS.

Father Mondiago will give the enclosed letters to the Dominican fathers if your Reverence is kind enough to ask him to deliver them.

AT eighteen years of age Teresa, of Old Castile, entered the Carmelite Order at Avila. She had frequent visions and ecstasies which helped to end those longings for the outer world which had hitherto haunted her. After twenty-five years of cloistered life, Teresa founded a house under the earlier and stricter Carmelite Rule in the same town, and then one for Discalced Friars of the same Rule at Durvello. Jealousies of the relaxed Carmelites caused her much persecution, but in 1580 her reformed houses were recognized as an independent Order by the Pope. Seventeen convents were founded by her before she died at Avila where her principal relics are enshrined. Her writings belong to the great Christian classics, and she is one of the great women of all time. Teresa of Avila loved to send and to receive letters, and she took particular pains over her own. She is in fact the Madame de Sévigné of the saints and she would have endorsed every word of what Lacondaire said of letter-writing: 'It is a very pleasing thing to write to those one loves; and if life was intended simply for the enjoyment of lawful pleasures, we should never tire, near or far, of conversing with those souls whose life forms part of our own.'

As her letters are so well known, we give above only a few short ones. The third letter was addressed to a confessor of the nuns, begging him not to give up hearing the sisters' confessions. The fourth is to an unknown lady, and was written in January, 1581. The last letter was also written in January, 1581, and was addressed to Mother Aña de la Encarnacion, Prioress of Salamanca.

St. Philip Neri

1515–1595

MY dearest daughter in the Lord,
I have been thinking of your name. Your name is María
and the gathering together of the waters (those great
reservoirs whence the rivers are supplied and to which they
return) are called in the Holy Scriptures in Latin 'Mária'
which is a little shorter than saying María. María is that
wonderful Virgin, that glorious Lady who conceived in
her womb and brought forth without prejudice to her
virginity, Him whom the whole expanse of heaven cannot
contain within itself—Christ the Son of God and of Mary.
This holy Mother of God is called the Star of the Sea
(Mare); wherefore I conclude that not without great mystery was this name given you, because in leaving the
world you were lifted by the hand of God from out of the
waters of that sea, in crossing which so vast a number of
miserable souls perish, and so few comparatively are
saved: and you, like another Peter, have been taken by the
hand and firmly held, so that you have walked, not through
the waters, but on them.

Now, my daughter, you have approached to the shore
of the Land of Promise, to that blessed country promised
to the elect of God, in which good religious will have so
high a place that they will be in the choir of the exalted
hierarchy with the Thrones; for those most happy spirits
are called the seat of God: and when St. Peter asked Christ
what reward they should receive for having left all things
and followed Him, He answered that they should sit upon

twelve seats with Him in that day when He should judge the world. The religious, therefore, having left all and followed Christ, Who has said that everyone who leaves his property and follows Him should be raised to that throne, we must conclude that at that great spectacle when the world shall be consumed with fire, and the trumpets of the angels shall sound, and when Lucifer and all the other demons and the damned shall fall into hell, that then, secure amidst these ruins and miseries, good religious, both men and women, who have kept their vows and rules, will be clothed with glory, and will triumph under the wings of the protection of Jesus Christ; and carnal and worldly men will say with confusion of face: 'See, those are they whom we despised, and we laughed at them, and thought them unhappy and foolish persons; but now they are with the angels on lofty thrones and seats of glory, and we fools and madmen are burning everlastingly in the inextinguishable fire of the abyss of hell!' Now since, my dearest daughter in Christ, you are within reach of so much happiness, do not turn back, but keeping away from the occasions of falling, and attaching yourself to good practices, a lover of your cell and of choir and of prayer, and above all of obedience and holy poverty, seek to gain the victory.

But in your mental prayers you must remember those who neither by boat nor by bridge are passing over this dangerous sea, but are fording it; and you ought to recommend them to the powerful and merciful Hand that succours you, and to have the greatest compassion for them and put them within your heart, just as they say that, amongst other properties, the pelican does when it wants to feed; for standing by the seashore it swallows some of those shells which pilgrims wear on their hats, and which are shut together like hard stones, and within them

133

is the oyster, and in the warmth of the stomach, the shell relaxes its firm hold of them and gradually opens; the pelican then vomits these shells, and so is nourished with the flesh of the oyster which was at first so firmly closed. Do you place these hard and obstinate sinners in your heart, and cry to God in your charity, and take some disciplines for them after you have asked leave to do so; and God will send them compunction, and will open their hearts to the light of grace, and you will obtain such a liking for this exercise, and will burn with such zeal for the conversion of souls, that you will melt into tears of sweetness while you think upon the joy there is in heaven to God and the angels in the conversion of a sinner; and you will so increase in charity and merit, and those souls converted by your prayers will be your glory and your crown, not that you have been the most powerful cause of their conversion but God, Who will give the fruit to you, reserving the honour only to Himself, since He has been the principal author of their conversion. Keep in good health and in the grace of God.

★

JESUS. MARIA.

I do not know whether I ought to call you dearest, as is usual at the beginning of letters, considering that because of the war, and your desire of keeping a whole skin, you have the heart to stay away from us all, from father, friends, and brothers. Good sons are wont to assist their father in his need with their substance, their strength, and their life . . . and there you are, so timid and anxious about yourself, when you ought to give anything for such an occasion of coming to receive, if need be, the crown of martyrdom. One may see from this that you have not as yet made a start, for death is wont to affright those only who are still in their sins, not those who, like St. Paul, habitually desire to die and to be with Christ. . . . Indeed, I may rather say that one of the greatest crosses that can be laid on a person such as I wish you to be is, the not dying for Christ, as perchance you might do if you were to come here. Anyone would like to stand on Mount Tabor and see Christ transfigured; but to go up to Jerusalem and to accompany Christ on Mount Calvary, few are willing. It is in the fire and in tribulations that the true Christian is known. For as to the consolations you had with Brother Alessio during your journey, there is nothing very wonderful in your having some joy in them, or in your shedding a few poor tears, and feeling some little glow of devotion, for Christ was drawing you with this gentle call to bear a little of the cross. Spiritual persons generally have sweetness first, and bitterness afterwards; therefore, shake off all lukewarmness, put away unreality, bear the cross, and do not make the cross bear you. Be, moreover, prudent and give no trouble to anyone; take care that others rather receive from you than you from them, for a spiritual man should have, only in order to give. If, as you write, you have met with so much humility and so much kindness, learn from this to be yourself humble and kind; and if the friend you praise so highly entertained you for nine days in Florence, because you had entertained him one day in Prato, remember that you are now bound to entertain him eighty-one days in Prato. But since for my misfortune, I have a secretary who can't see anything, and has such a bad memory as to make Solomon himself talk nonsense, I must draw to a close, all the more as I am ill in bed, visited by the Lord. . . . Commend me to Sister Catherine [de Ricci], and beg her to pray God for me that I may win many souls, and that I may not bury in the earth the talents given

135

me, be they five or ten, three or one. Pray for me, for I am sick in body, and not as I could wish to be in my soul.

*

THE mole is a blind animal which abides always in the earth; it eats earth and burrows in earth, and is never satiated with earth. And such is the avaricious man or woman; women are by nature avaricious. And what a revolting thing is avarice! A man has received so much from God—he has given him, besides his being, and all created things from the angels downwards, his own Son. The sweet Christ, the Incarnate Word, gave himself to us, without reserve, even to the hard and shameful death of the Cross, and then gave himself to us in a Sacrament, as at first he left heaven, humbling himself to become man for us; and on the Cross he was stripped of his garments, and shed his precious Blood, and his soul was separated from his body. All things created are open-hearted and liberal, and show forth the goodness of their Creator; the sun pours abroad light, and fire gives out heat; every tree stretches forth its arms and reaches to us its fruit; the water and the air, and all nature, declare the bounty of the Creator. And we, who are yet his living images, we do not represent him, but with base degeneracy deny him in our works, however much we confess him with our mouths. Now, if avarice is a monstrous thing in any man, what is it in a religious who has made a vow of poverty, abandoning everything for the love of God! We must, at whatever cost of pain, get rid of this foul pestilence of avarice; nor shall we feel the pain if we seriously reflect that as soon as we cast off this sordid garb, our soul is clothed with a regal and imperial garment. I mean not only that we must despise gold and silver and pleasure and all else that is so prized by a blind, deluded world, but that we are to give even the very life we love so much for the honour of God and the salvation of our neighbour, having our hearts ever ready to make this sacrifice, in the strength of divine grace.

ST. PHILIP NERI, founder of the Congregation of the Oratory in Italy, was born at Florence in 1515, and from his childhood led a blameless life. His father, who was a lawyer, gave him an excellent education, and sent him into the counting-house of his uncle at San Germano, at the foot of Monte Cassino; but Philip felt that he had no vocation for a commercial life, and he left for Rome, where he studied philosophy and canon law. In time he became well-known for his learning, and was consulted by those who had been his masters. Resolving to devote himself only to the service of God and the salvation of souls, he sold his books, distributed the money to the poor, and spent his time in the hospitals, or in going among the worldly and irreligious, endeavouring to reclaim them. In 1548 he formed, with fourteen companions, a Congregation attached to the church of St. Salvatore-del-Campo. Two years after, he transferred it to the church of the Trinità, and erected a hospital in connexion with it, which still exists. His humility held him back from approaching the priesthood until he was thirty-six years of age, when, in obedience to his Director but with much distrust of himself, he was ordained priest.

He then associated himself with a small community of priests who were attached to the church of St. Jerome. St. Philip lived with undimmed intellect to the age of eighty, expiring just after midnight, between the 25th and the 26th of May, 1595. He was called, even in his lifetime, the Apostle of Rome.

The first letter was addressed to a religious, the second to Francis Vai, dated 6th November, 1556, and the third to his niece, a nun.

St. Peter Canisius

1521–1597

I SEE that God has been pleased to surround your Reverence with infirmity. But though you are not always able to pull the chariot of the body with the same vigour, you have at least the comfort in Our Lord of many companions to sustain and protect the slow and burdened vehicle. Your inability is the lot of many men, and to a Christian it can never seem strange; so why, I beg you, should we be chagrined? Have we not reached the stage where this life ought to have lost its edge of delight for us, and the passage to true life, its fears? Meantime, may your charity find its viaticum, by which you may be strengthened and set straight however much bodily powers fail and dread of death takes possession; the viaticum, I mean, of a lively feeling of the Passion of Our Lord. Let us bring before our eyes the blood and wounds of Christ, His sweat, His Cross, and His death. Let us with true and ardent faith rest in Christ crucified, drinking the waters of life from that fountain, glorying in His merits and rejoicing heartily that whether we live or die He is our life and resurrection, our Head and the propitiation for our sins. But I must stop preaching. The Lord will give as He has given your Reverence understanding to meditate on these truths in season, and to derive from them the profit of consolation which they contain.

★

DEAREST Brothers in Christ Our Lord, may the grace

of the Holy Spirit, peace past all understanding and the immortal fruits of obedience be yours. Your letter reached me this very evening, good evidence not only of your diligence and progress in study but of your charity and courtesy to me, your brother. What could be pleasanter news for me and for all of us here than to learn of your undisguised contempt for worldly vanities, of your united ardour in bearing the yoke of Christ, of your strong determination to fulfil the precepts of obedience, and, finally, of the wonderful holy rivalry wherewith you pursue your studies and foster in your souls those desires which Christ suggests to His chosen ones?

Though, I think, you have no need of my exhortations, I nevertheless beg and implore you all, through Our Lord Jesus Christ, to prize obedience as the most beautiful and most holy of services and to bring into relation with it every detail of your studies and every movement of your hearts. For family love, learning, sermons, prayers, and all holy exercises ought to have their place and importance in our lives determined for us by their conformity with obedience. Anything that openly withdraws us from obedience, or causes us to be unfaithful to it in secret, profanes the temple of God, grieves His Holy Spirit, defeats His love and makes progress in all true religion impossible.

I would wish, then, that, as a rock-like foundation for your lives, you should daily consider with attentive hearts this your divine vocation, asking yourselves whether there is anything you ought to make good or improve in it, in order to be truly the companions of Jesus and to be justly so esteemed. . . . To this are you called, Brothers, for this are you ordained that you should in accordance with the simple rule of obedience surrender and resign yourselves to the guidance of another in all things, for the love of Christ.

If you do this, as by divine and human sanction you should, then reckon yourselves novices, soldiers, brothers, disciples of the Society of Jesus; then judge that all is well with you, though there be few who approve the way you have chosen, nay, though everybody should neglect you utterly and visit you with their hate and scorn. . . .

I am sending you the records of what seem to me the most beautiful fruits of obedience which the Captain of our Army, Jesus, gathered from His soldiers only a few months ago. How true it is that the hand of the Lord is not shortened! You will read in these letters about your brothers' most gallant struggles, about their burning zeal, their indefatigable labours, their apostolic faith, and their neighbourly charity, so great as hardly to be believed. And all this structure of God was built on the foundation of obedience. I shall be surprised indeed if you can read the story of such wonderful and perfect doings without profit to your souls. For myself, I was profoundly affected and felt myself quite a changed man, especially when I measured my meanness against the glorious example of my brethren.

We must pray to the Father of mercies that He may always keep us and our Society what it has so happily been from its beginning, namely, the good odour of Christ in almost every place, not only in Italy, Sicily, Spain, and Portugal, but in Arabia, India, and other regions where the holy name of Christ had hitherto been unknown. Of Germany I need not now say anything, though this land, too, has seen the Society's labours and will see them more and more as time goes on. Here in Ingoldstadt many things promise well for us, even though the old Duke of Bavaria be dead. . . .

It was a great pleasure to receive from you the greetings of my Fathers of the Charterhouse. I am most anxious that you should remember me to them in turn. I shall not let pass any occasion of serving such excellent men, though, in truth, it is rather Canisius who needs the help of their prayers, Canisius whom they took so readily and kindlily to their hearts for many years that they deserve to be held dearer by him than all his dear ones. . . .

Good-bye, beloved Brothers, and continue to pray very much for us because of our great need.

*

MY Brothers in Christ, dear and desired, I have so much to tell you, so many things glad and sad to say, that I scarcely know how to begin my letter. It is a very sweet experience when a man folds his friend to his heart and looks upon his face again, especially when that friend has come from far away bringing with him the expectation and ardent desires of many a month. So, too, men cannot help feeling a certain corresponding sadness when they have reason to believe that the long-sought means and opportunities to improve their friendships may be removed from them, not for a time only but for good. In this way I think it is possible that both you and I may find some small trouble taking possession of our souls, you at seeing your old friend Canisius, the one man you knew in Rome, spirited suddenly far away from you just as you arrived in the City, and I, because deprived of the chance to welcome my eagerly awaited brothers, among the first of our Society's sons from Germany, after their long and arduous journey. . . . That journey, however, had a happy end, for it placed you in the centre of all that is mighty and magnificent in the world and gave you, as you now know, the best of fathers and the truest of brothers to delight your hearts. It seems to me that such an exchange might well make us forget our unhappy Germany and give our

141

undivided love to the City which has ever kept inviolate the faith of Christ and Peter, and which now bestows on us a new happiness, excelling immeasurably whatever delight there is in the pomp of the world or the gratification of sense. . . . In this new school you learn the abundant riches of poverty, the true freedom of obedience, the glory of humility and the supreme dignity and worth of the love of Jesus crucified. . . .

As for the solid development of our friendship, we must not measure that by our nearness to one another in the flesh, which is a mean and vulgar standard, for it consists rather in likeness of soul and harmony of will. Since, then, our endeavours to serve Christ are of one pattern and our ways of life very similar, how can we, with the breath of the Holy Spirit upon us, be anything but united wherever we are? How can the miles between us sunder our souls, or ever silence the converse of heart with heart? And then if we would think of the perfect union, may we not cherish the hope and desire, brothers, of going home together after this brief circle of years to the happy, happy country where death is dead and evil has no power to harm, where the Eternal Father waits to fill us with all delight, and where our beatitude will be crowned in the company of the brothers we loved so dearly? . . .

CANISIUS was born in 1521 at Nijmwegen. At the age of fifteen, Peter entered the University of Cologne, where he formed a close friendship with a saintly and sympathetic priest, Nikolaus van Esch. When eighteen, he pledged himself to a life of celibacy, and prayed the Lord to 'show me Thy ways and teach me to walk in them'

He made the Spiritual Exercises for thirty days under Father Peter Faer, one of the original companions of St. Ignatius, and on 8th May, 1543, entered the lately established novitiate at Cologne, the first of his countrymen to do so.

Before leaving Rome, in 1549, he was solemnly professed in the Society in the church of Sancta Maria della Strada, the Mass on this occasion being celebrated by St. Ignatius. He won over the apathetic and ill-read students by his kindness and devotion to their interests, assisted the poorer sort by financial help, and explained the nature of the interior life as expressed in the Spiritual Exercises.

The year that St. Ignatius died (1556), Canisius was appointed Provincial of the Society in South Germany, and during the years that he held this very important office, he achieved a series of triumphs which may be described as Napoleonic.

To dam one tide of loss at its source Fr. Canisius drew up an excellent 'Catechism' which appeared in April, 1555. The larger and Latin version was used with splendid effect in all the Catholic schools and by many of the parochial clergy. An abridgement in the vernacular was soon issued for children in the ordinary schools, where it has an enormous vogue. The larger Catechism (Latin) was enlarged into a serious handbook of theology in 1569, and it went through no fewer than 200 editions during the writer's lifetime. It contains some 3,200 references to Scripture passages and the Fathers.

Seminaries and colleges were improved or founded by his care, and St. Peter Canisius made it possible for Macaulay to declare when writing nearly three centuries later that 'a hundred years after the separation [from Rome] Protestantism could scarcely maintain itself on the shores of the Baltic'.

He appeared in the pulpit at Freiburg for the last time in 1596, on the occasion of the opening of a new College, but was then described as 'worn out with years and work'.

His amazing energy and prudence revived the zeal of the Catholic princes and bishops, reformed the universities, and brought whole cities and provinces back to the Church. He defended the Faith in imperial diets against worldly statesmen, and in public conferences against the leaders of heresy. After assisting at the Council of Trent, he went as Apostolic Nuncio to promote the execution of its decrees in Germany, Bohemia, Poland, and Austria. He died with every mark of sanctity at Freiburg in 1597.

St. Catherine of Ricci

1522–1590

MOST honoured and dearly-loved Father, greeting!

Two days ago, I wrote you what was necessary about Cassandra: that is, that she had rather you would leave her here until she sends you notice; so that, in talking to her yesterday evening, I said: 'Cassandra, I am afraid that, as your father has been asked to leave you here, if we say nothing more to him he will suspect something, and come to fetch you as soon as possible.' She replied: 'I would on no account have him come for me yet. As to becoming a nun, I wish to do so; but I don't wish to speak about it to the sisters without having told him first.' Then I said: 'I don't think he will let you do it.' 'And I,' she answered, 'believe that he will let me do what I please; but I would rather not go home so soon, so as to have too many struggles there, especially with Lucrezia.' She also told Sister Maria Pia that she has determined to be a nun, but one can see that she wants to stay here just a little longer, so as to strengthen her soul, and also that she wants you to be told first of her resolution. Therefore, if you can leave her to us for another eight or ten days, I should think it a great advantage.

Be sure, my dear Father, that nobody here has ever said one word to influence her: she has been allowed to see everything connected with the Order, and with our observances, and we have noticed that she has paid great attention to it all; but the fact of her desire comes from

Jesus Himself; He would have that soul entirely. I want, then, to encourage you not to take it from Him; for certainly you will have more real satisfaction in giving your daughter to our Lord for His own, than you would in refusing her to Him only to give her to a mortal spouse, subject to all the miseries of this life. Even if some fuss should be made about the matter, you ought not for that reason to act against your duty; for as you know, the things of God must always meet with opposition, especially when they clash with earthly plans. I think it would be well, when you come here, not to let Cassandra see that you know anything, but to let her be the first to speak, so as to give you her confidence spontaneously. Moreover, I think myself that you had better not discuss the matter with anyone: but this I must leave to your own judgement. We do not forget, here, to pray that all may be ordered by our Lord for both your daughter's salvation and your satisfaction.

Mother Maria Maddalena (Strozzi), from fear of you, sent you word yesterday that I had an attack of fever; but do not think I am ill, as, to judge by present symptoms, the fit has passed and I do not think it will return.

My best greetings to you, to Mona Maria, and to all. May God keep you!

Mother Prioress commends herself to you,

Your daughter,

SISTER CATHERINE DE' RICCI

★

I HAVE received your most welcome letter. . . .

You tell me you do not feel well, and I quite believe it although I do not see what can be done. I would however remind you that we shall, hereafter, have to give an account for our indiscretion as well as for our superfluous care of ourselves. I wish that you would not do things beyond your strength: you will injure yourself irreparably. For instance you ought not to have gone from here. You were told so often enough, but you only answered: 'Whether it snow, or whether it hail, go I will.' It is useless to argue with a man who has made up his mind, and you were determined to go, come what might . . . although I was very sorry to hear it and would, had I been able, have kept every drop from falling on your dear head. But you would not obey me who am so full of good wishes towards you. Then came your carriage accident and your difficulty in getting home. Surely it would have been more pleasing to Jesus had you remained at home instead of going whither you went. I do not mean that He is displeased if we suffer in doing right for love of Him: on the contrary, this is most acceptable to Him as long as we keep within the limits of prudence and reason. We shall nevertheless be judged for indiscretion, but on this point I will say no more.

Here we are at nine o'clock on Tuesday evening, and I think you must have ended your day and gone to rest. I assure you that this weather is most unfavourable to your health, so I beg of you to be content to take some care of yourself at least until the middle of April. Do this for the love of Jesus and for the sake of your daughters and in order to gain time during which you may work for God, for this indeed ought to be our aim.

The jubilee has passed and we thank Lorenzo for it: I am very glad to have had it.

I do not know how to express myself more clearly about the cell than I have done in my other letter. Sister Fede Vittoria prefers it small and does not think of the objection which I pointed out to you, viz., that in stormy weather she is frightened and must have a sister with her, and it would not be agreeable for two to remain for some days in a small cell until she be reassured. . . . But if you will make it as you think best, all difficulties will be at an end.

I have received the wine and some of it was given me at collation last night after I had read your letter, for my throat had swollen very much on hearing of your troubles. But your news was so bitter that I could not taste the sweetness of the wine. However this morning I found it sweet, and I thank you for it.

Last night and this morning I remembered you and offered to Jesus your body, soul and heart, your memory, understanding and will. They are like six water pots and I implored Him to change their water into wine. I prayed that, as wine purifies and preserves, so your mind may be purified from all that disturbs it and your good will preserved by means of good works. I beg of you to be likewise mindful of me and to pray for me.

I commend myself to you, and so does Mother Prioress. Mother Margherita and Sister Maddalena also wish to be remembered to you, and the latter sends a greeting likewise to her Toto.

I think I will send Niccolino to see you, for I shall not be happy until I hear that you are well after your misadventures.

*

NOW that you are at Florence, I fear nobody will think of giving you broth and biscuit for supper; and therefore I send you a basket of chestnuts, so that you may eat at least four every evening. I would remind you that Jesus wishes us to keep the mean, not the extreme, in our lives; and to use reasonable human methods of preserving health. . . .

147

We are not to aim at dying but at living to do good, and so to honour and glorify God in ourselves.

I understand that you go to hear sermons and like them. I wish that instead of going for them to St. Peter's you would come here. But I should not like the distance to be a trouble to you, only an additional merit. If you came here we might meet when it was convenient. I look forward to the day when we shall see each other, not at St. Peter's, nor here, nor at Florence nor Prato, but in heaven, in the fruition of Jesus and His holy Mother and the whole celestial court.

*

I HAVE received your welcome letter, but did I not think that there was some of your sister Bernarda's mischief in it I should be vexed at it. To tell you the truth I do not believe that you mean what you say when you tell me of such grievances, for I know that I never more heartily wished you well than I do now and I have never had a moment's disturbance on account of you. It seems to me that you have done more for our brethren than their own father would have done. Now as I know that my feeling towards you has not changed, but is as undoubted as when I impressed upon you the duty of desiring to please our Lord and to be wholly His, I would fain think that in what you say you are speaking not in earnest but in jest. . . . But, my father, if you should indeed have such an idea in your head, I beg of you to dismiss it, for it is utterly ground-less. God knows how heartily I wish you well and how constantly I pray to the holy angels and to your guardian angel to give you a place in heaven. But if you have any doubt on the subject they will make all clear to you during this festival. When my dear father was alive I do not think that I ever forgot him or ever thought of him without wishing him this same happiness. Jesus has given you to me both father and son, could I be so mistaken as to esteem lightly that which it has taken me so many years to obtain from God? Would such be your conduct? I think not; and, even were you to act so, I most certainly should not. Never will I let go of your soul; be sure of that, my naughty friend. This must suffice without an oath, for I must not be long as I have taken Sister Bernarda away from the washing, and she says that the sun is very hot, for it is late, ten o'clock already.

I am happy to hear that the sisters and the children are well, for I love them as long as they are good. I am still more glad that you are sending them back tomorrow or the next day. I shall regret it very much if, as I fear, they have given you trouble. You have an opportunity of sending them to me and you will see how gladly I shall make the exchange. Say this to Mona Maria, and make my excuses to her for sending her such a number at a time, as if she had not children enough already. I thank both you and her for the very great enjoyment which you have given them. . . . Mother Prioress and Mother M. Maddalena desire to be remembered to you: they say that Toto must not be left behind.

I would have sent Salvadore with the mule for the children, but as you forbid me to do so I will obey you. I will expect them at the hour you mention. . . . Farewell.

*

I WOULD remind you, my dear Father, that when the man who owned 10,000 talents asked his Master to forgive his debt, he did not beg the favour for 9,000 only, but for the whole sum. If this debtor had not acted afresh with hardness and cruelty he would have had nothing to fear about the past debt, as it had been fully and freely remitted; and his Lord would have been actually offended if the servant had not believed simply in the pardon granted to him. . . . Hence I conclude that, although it be a great error to count presumptuously on oneself, we nevertheless greatly offend the mercy and goodness of God by distrust. We know that He is very generous: that He became man and suffered a painful passion and death to deliver us from all anxiety as to our salvation; and that, by these acts, He has opened heaven to us, provided we do not ourselves turn in the opposite direction. In the latter case, there can be no uncertainty, as most assuredly he who does not act according to the law of Jesus cannot reach heaven, any more than a man who takes the road to Pistoja when he wants to go to Florence can expect to arrive at Florence! But, so long as he takes *one* of the three roads that lead to Florence—even though he may find he has taken the worst one, with a good many bad bits that will hinder him—if he gives his horse the rein and goes on steadily, he may expect certainly to get there at last. So one may find in the right way to heaven many hindrances that are serious obstacles; but for these there is the remedy given by Jesus: namely, to walk by the light that will lead us safely, and that light is holy faith. If we will only walk with our eyes fixed on this, we shall see before us a road, clear, level, beautiful, and very pleasant to walk upon; shaded, too, by the green leaves of hope, planted with the flowers of holy longings, and abounding in the fruits of good works. By following this road, we shall go straight to our true home. Hence, whoever yields to fear or dread on this way insults his Lord and Master, or that Master's representative who acts as His guarantee. Of course, when you say that you have kept back something to tell me *viva voce*, I am writing partly in the dark; but I can safely assure you that, when we have once plunged thoroughly into that fiery furnace [of sorrow and penance] all our spots and stains are consumed. ... What use is it then, dear Father, to be afraid? Of what use, I repeat, except to make us lose time on the way, and walk with but little fervour towards Jerusalem? So let us drive away fear, and put in its stead holy hope: but a hope without presumption, and founded on the goodness of God, not on our own merits.

★

I KNOW that Sister Maria Maddalena has written fully to you about me in the letter which she sent you this morning by a labourer. She has told you that my fever came on last evening with great intensity, accompanied by headache and violent sweating. It lasted all night until past seven this morning, but today I seem to be better than I was on Friday morning. Now however it is nearly nine o'clock in the evening and I am beginning to have the same inflammation that I had last night. I do not know whether it is a symptom of the return of my fever. But it is a slight thing, and I am in good hopes that by the help of Jesus I shall soon be well, especially if you will come to see me when you can. One good sign of my improvement is that whereas hitherto I have not been able to think of anything connected with my work, I am today building little castles in the air about flax spinning. Sister Maddalena laughs and tells me that a doctor told her in another illness of mine that when I began to think about certain things it was a sign that nature was beginning to be freed from sickness and to return to its normal state. I tell you this for your satisfaction, and because I do not wish you to be any longer uneasy about me.

I, my dear father, am kept under such strict obedience

that sometimes I lift up my head a little to see whether I be alive at all. I could get up and go about but I cannot succeed in doing it. I assure you that if the Bolognese honey changed its flavour as much as my mother has changed, apothecaries would no longer sell it as sweet or even as half sweet. If I am ever dispensed from this rigorous obedience I shall think myself fortunate. For pity's sake do not make my mother more despotic with me than she already is, for she is very masterful and I can no longer send her to supper nor to bed. She will have nothing of the sort, and merely answers: 'You must obey your father,' and thus shuts my mouth so that I can say no more. For my further comfort she has even induced the doctor to say that I am not to be in my cell. Now if you will help me with your prayers, I hope that soon I shall do as much as you tell me, to be avenged if not on the doctor at least on my mother.

Sister Valeria and the other nuns thank you for the chick-peas. There are plenty of them because they mix well with other vegetables: they furnish a dessert.

Tomorrow at Mass (for I hear it from my bed) I shall not fail to remember you and to commend you to Jesus and to those two holy apostles who will, I hope, be with you when you go to the coming fair. My greetings to you and to Mona Maria. . . .

Thank you for the pears, and the honey, and the grapes: you do too much for me. Sister Bernarda does not think it worth while to write. She never leaves me save to write to you; she bids me remember her to you.

*

I AM full of confusion when I think that you, who are occupied without ceasing in so many great things for the glory of God, should set yourself to write to me who am only a weak woman of no value, and a miserable sinner. May God reward you for the great charity you do me! I asked the Lord that I might be able to serve Him this Lent in health of body; and He granted me this grace in such wise that I found myself suddenly and completely cured, though it seems to me that I have done nothing to merit this. I have, nevertheless, made over to you a part of all I do, and I have besought His divine Majesty to restore and preserve your health, because Holy Church has so great need of you. I beg you to pray to Jesus for me, that the many graces he bestows on me every moment be not thrown away through my fault. In regard of your death be of good cheer; for to a servant so faithful as you have been all through the course of your life, God, who is ever most just, cannot refuse the reward of Paradise. Prostrate on the ground I implore your holy blessing.

*

THIS holy Mother of God is called the Star of the sea; wherefore I conclude that not without deep meaning was this name given you, because drawn from the waters of that sea, in crossing which so many hapless souls perish, the greater part sunk deep in the waters, and few comparatively escape. But you, like another Peter, have been taken by the hand and upheld, so that you have not so much walked through the waters as upon them. Those holy fathers of the Old Testament walked through the midst of the waters and were not drowned. You know how the Red Sea was parted, and the river Jordan, so that by the grace of God the people passed through the waters unharmed. But the Christian Church walks upon the waves of the sea, and does not even wet her feet, if she abide steadfast in the faith, following in the footsteps of her lawful

Spouse and Guide. The walking of those patriarchs of old time through the midst of the waters means that, possessing riches and having wives and children, they lived without soiling their affections with any of these things; for they took of them only the use, and were ready to leave them at the bidding of God.

. . . . Holy Peter and the other apostles, and apostolic men after them, and all that primitive Church in Jerusalem, when they saw the Son of God born in poverty and living in poverty, with nothing of His own, so that He had not even where to lay His head, and beheld Him dead and naked on a cross, stripped themselves of everything, desiring only what might cover them decently and sustain them poorly in extreme necessity; and they chose the way of the counsels, as do in this day all true religious, who keep ever living within them the image and exemplar of that most wondrous foundation of Christian perfection; relinquishing not only the possession of property and all else that they might with a good conscience keep, but also their own opinion and notions and will, in order that they may have a perfect victory over themselves, and that the kingdom of Christ may come to bear rule in their souls with His grace and His love, and that the devil may be banished thence, and never more have sway therein by means of sin. Now, my daughter, you have with your little bark almost reached the shore of the land of promise, that blessed country promised to the elect of God . . . The Holy Spirit speaks to you thus in the psalm: Listen, O daughter, and from the words receive light and effulgence of grace, and in that light look around you. When you see the fair and peaceful land that is pointed out to you, forget that other land full of toil and weariness, which brings forth only thorns and briars; have no memory more of your country and your father's house, but incline the ear of obedience to my words, and stoop your shoulder to the cross of true mortification, exterior and interior both, of all evil ways and thoughts and all delusive loves. Put in Me thy trust, thy hope, and all thy affection; so will I take thee for My bride, and have delight in thy modesty and humility. I will give thee from My table every manner of food I am wont to give to those who serve and love Me faithfully, such as the temptations I permit, and tribulations which at first will seem to thee bitter, but after, when thou growest used to them, will be sweet to thy taste. And thou wilt learn and know that this way, the way I take with those I love, is the true espousal of thy soul to Me.

ALEXANDRINA OF RICCI was the daughter of a Florentine noble. At the age of thirteen she entered the Third Order of St. Dominic in the monastery of Prato, taking in religion the name of Catherine, after her patron and namesake of Siena, and was prioress from 1560 until her death. Her special attraction was to the Passion of Christ, in which she was permitted miraculously to participate. In Lent when she was twenty-one years of age, she had a vision of the Crucifixion so heartrending that she was confined to bed for three weeks, and was only restored on Holy Saturday, by an apparition of St. Mary Magdalen and the risen Christ. During twelve years she passed every Friday in ecstasy. All these favours gave her continual and intense suffering, and inspired her with a loving sympathy for the yet more bitter tortures of the Holy Souls. On their behalf she offered all her prayers and penances; and her charity towards them became so famous throughout Tuscany, that after every death the friends of the deceased hastened to Catherine to secure her prayers. She died at Prato amid angels' songs, in 1590. She is said to have received from Christ the ring of espousals and the stigmata. Her ecstatic life and the gift of miracles brought her into contact with St. Philip Neri.

The first letter was written to Filippo Salviato from Prato on 4th July, 1560, the second on 6th January, 1561, and the third on

12th February, 1561. The next letter was addressed to Valdimarina, 24th September, 1561, where the sisters and girls from San Vincenzio were then staying. The fifth was written on 2nd October, 1561, in reply to some spiritual troubles, and doubts about his salvation, communicated to her by Filippo. The sixth letter was addressed to Valdimarina, 27th October, 1561.

St. Louis Bertrand

1526–1581

MY much honoured Father,
        I know full well that you and my mother
will feel sorry at my present design, but that sorrow ought
not to continue when you know that it is the will of God
that I should thus leave you.

Probably you will ask, How do we know that such is
God's will? In answer, you will readily understand that I
should never have broken off my studies and started off
alone in the midst of the winter's cold unless I had felt
powerfully drawn to do so by God's call. And let not the
thought of what I have to suffer distress you, for you must
remember that our Redeemer came down from heaven,
and was born in the coldest season of the year, and that He
came to die in order to give ungrateful sinners life. How
much more, then, ought I, sinner as I am, to leave the world
and to go whithersoever His Majesty calls me, to do penance for my many sins against God?

I know that my departure will occasion you more sorrow on account of the illness of my mother, but she ought
to be comforted by remembering what holy writers say
about the happiness of the soul that is afflicted in this world;
how its trials are a sign that the eyes of God's tender mercy
are turned upon it, and that He intends to reward in glory
the good works it does here below. Some people have the
good they perform rewarded here, while the evil they fall
into is punished in the next world. Therefore this trial is to
be accepted with patience; and you should pray that the

Divine Majesty may ever support me with His holy Hand, may conduct me as He did Magdalen, and may defend me always from the snares of the enemy.

I have borrowed a little money from—— [certain people mentioned]. This money I have no intention of spending in pleasure-seeking, but I thought I might need a small sum as a means of support, in case God should please to visit me with illness in punishment for my sins, although His Divine Majesty Himself is the best help and medicine in all maladies. I beg you, my father, to restore this little sum to its owners, that my conscience may be easy.

I beseech you not to try to discover where I am, for I think you would not succeed; and even if you did find me, I hope that my God and Master, Jesus, would preserve me firmly in my resolution. I beg you to commend me to His Divine Mother, and to pray that she may guide me to the place in which I can best serve her Son.

Lastly, I implore you to try and console my mother. Remind her that she has other children to be a comfort to her, and tell her to imagine that I was taken away by death in my infancy.

Nothing more will I add, except an earnest prayer that the Father, Son, and Holy Ghost may be with you, my parents, may ever help you, and be with me. Amen. May the grace be given us to serve God in this life, and in the next to rejoice in eternal rest!

ST. LOUIS was born at Valencia, in Spain, and after joining the Dominicans, was sent to preach the gospel in South America in 1562. He worked in what is now Colombia for seven years, making numerous converts among the Indians both there and in some of the West Indian islands. On his return to Spain, St. Louis achieved fame as a preacher and was active in keeping up the primitive spirit of his Order. He died in 1581 in the town of his birth, and was canonized in 1671.

St. Alphonsus Rodriguez

1531–1617

Pax Christi.

My very dear Father, so great is my lowliness
that I should not have ventured to write this, unworthy as
I am to speak to your Paternity. However, as holy obedience has ordered me to do so, I do so. It seems to me a
piece of boldness for a poor old broken-down Brother like
myself to address your Paternity. However, as God has, by
obedience, ordered me to do so, and as it is His holy will, I
affirm that the captivity of our Fathers and Brothers is not
to be looked upon as a misfortune, but as good fortune;
not as adversity, but as prosperity; not as trouble, but as
comfort and repose; and they themselves will hereafter
recognize this better, from the great good that they will
have drawn from this tribulation, and they will see what a
favour God has done them in allowing them to be carried
away prisoners to Algiers, for the glory of God and the
salvation of souls who are living there, and for their own,
with the grace of God. In the Missions hereabouts there is
no danger of denying one's Faith; while in Algiers there is.
And thus it is a great act of charity to aid them [the Alger-
ians] with the help of ours and the grace of God. Therefore we ought to look upon this trouble as a piece of good
fortune, which has come from the hand of God, and not as
a misfortune. And this, merely on account of the great
good which has come from it, and will still come from it,
as is already known from the letters of one of the Fathers.
Fortunate mission! sent forth, not by the hands of men,

but by God Himself; and if for no other reason, to encourage those souls who are in danger of denying their Faith and of so being lost. It is a great treasure for them, and for those too who aid them, because this is the way that God wishes that they should be aided and saved. Besides, at what price can we value this immense good and treasure of salvation, and the share of grace and glory which will come to ours from this [suffering for God]? Who can tell how great is this treasure which ours have there obtained?

This will prove a source not only of increase to the Society, but will add to its esteem, and will further it in its charity and love both of God and of its neighbour. The Society has gone to India, and will leave it enriched with the treasures of God, both for itself and for many; and so too these adversities, as they are called by a deluded world, are nevertheless, in the eyes of the servants of God, who are enlightened with His light, a real good fortune, gifts of God, and great favours.

At the outset of this affair I felt some grief according to the flesh, because I did not catch what was the end which God had in this trial. Afterwards, however, when I came to understand by a special light what had happened to ours, I was consoled and pacified, for I saw that men cannot perceive whither tend the actions of God; for if we did, we should console ourselves, and whatever might come from His hands, we should bear it for His sake. For, with the wonderful love with which He loves us, He ever guards us and turns all that concerns us to His greater glory and to the good of our souls.

It is one thing to see our troubles with the eyes of the world and of the flesh; but far different to see them in the spiritual light according to God, and not according to the flesh, accepting everything as from the hands of God, and not as from those of His creatures or of the devils; rejoicing at everything, and blessing and thanking God for the favours bestowed, and saying in all that happens, whether for us or against us, 'Non mea, sed Tua voluntas fiat'; or, with St. Paul, prostrate at the feet of Christ: 'Domine, quid me vis facere?—Behold me here at Thy bidding.' God willed that Jonas should preach to the city of Ninive in order that it might do penance for its sins; but Jonas did not wish to go there, and God placed him in Ninive, though much against his will. So, too, ours did not wish to go to Algiers; but God wished that they should go there to aid those souls which were in need of aid. And so He sent them to Algiers, as another Jonas to Ninive, where they are reaping great fruit for souls with God's grace.

The way of the cross by trials suffered for God is the way to Heaven, and there is a greater difference between adversity suffered for God and prosperity, even in holy things, than there is between a piece of lead and all the gold in the world. And yet for all this, to suffer for Christ, in spite of its great price, is not loved by all; while what the world calls prosperity, that is of the body, is esteemed and loved and sought after at the cost of great toil. Prosperity, according to the flesh, blinds us with self-love and puffs us up. Adversity rouses us to go to God and to look to ourselves. By means of adversities and tribulations, through the grace of God, a man becomes spiritual and holy; he is made an imitator of Christ our Lord, for it is by their means that he attains sanctity. Through adversities and trials suffered for God, he merits before God great degrees of grace and glory, and his soul can say: 'Then I am best when I am worst'; that is to say, when I have most troubles; and thus, 'per multas tribulationes oportet introire in regnum Dei'.

I commend myself earnestly to your Paternity's holy sacrifices and prayers.

★

TAKE heed that neither this virtue, nor any other, consists in mere talk, or saying high things about humility; for many know a great deal about it, who yet have no humility at all. But it consists in having it deeply planted and fixed in the heart, and that is why our Lord said: 'Learn of Me, for I am meek and humble of heart.' Thus he gives us to understand that humility, as every virtue, has its dwelling, its throne, in the heart, and not in the tongue. So that it is not to be acquired by saying marvellous things about it, which is easy enough, but by fixing and planting it deep in the heart by blows of the hammer of mortification, by victories over self, and by casting out all pride and high thoughts so completely as to come to relish all contempt and dishonour, a thing which costs us dear.

The road to this self-knowledge is by meditating on various truths, natural and revealed, which shows us what we really are.

First—Our absolute nothing. 'He who thinks himself to be something, whereas he is nothing, deceives himself', Gal. vi, 3. We now are, as far as ourselves are concerned, no more than we were a century back—as incapable of any good now as we were then, if God did not come to our aid. Our soul is nothing, knows nothing, can do nothing, is capable of nothing, is worth nothing.

And this shows us clearly that we have our being, not in order to work, or to do anything merely for itself, because God alone is a Being uncreated and self-existing, and who therefore alone can work for Himself. A secondary cause can do nothing save by the first—which is God. 'All things are made by Him, and without Him there is nothing', John i, 3.

We learn this clearly in time of temptation, for we find we have not a particle of strength, except what comes from Heaven. When they told St. Francis that he was holy and did holy actions, his answer was: 'I do nothing that is good'; for he attributed all good to God, Who gives us even the will to do good, and we are merely the instruments with which God does what He pleases, and without Whom we could do nothing—just as it is the scribe, and not the pen, who writes; but he writes with the pen—for an instrument never does anything by itself, neither can it. So, neither more nor less, can we do anything good, except through God, nor can we bear anything so as to please him, for He is what He is, and we are what we are. And this was why, when Judith cut off the head of Holofernes, she said: 'God has cut off the head of Holofernes by the hand of a woman.' St. Paul and St. Catherine of Siena thoroughly realized this our weakness, when tempted; but the Lord gave them strength by speaking to them; and Elias felt it too, when fleeing from Jezebel.

The second consideration must be to think before God how wicked the soul has been against a Lord so good as is its Creator, from whom it has received its very being, and favours without number. So that it may know how little it is worth, because of the multitude and gravity of its sins. At the sight of them it should always be filled with a humble fear, despising and detesting itself for its treasons and crimes against its God, Whom it has repaid with such wrongs for favours so great and so grand which it has received from His Divine Majesty.

The third consideration is to see how destitute is the soul as if it were not, for it has nothing good in itself, but all is from God. For God alone is good, God alone is holy, and not man, except so far as God gives him to be so.

ALPHONSUS RODRIGUEZ, who for the greater part of a century instructed and edified so many persons, was not a priest, or eminent theologian, but a simple lay-brother of the Society of

Jesus. Born at Segòvia, Spain, of devout parents of the commercial class, Diego and María Rodriguez, on 25th July, 1531, he early displayed remarkable devotion to Our Lady. As a little child, he loved to kiss her pictures and images, yet it is said that he was twelve years of age before he was instructed in the devotion to which he was always so attached, i.e., that of the rosary. He studied at the Universities of Alcalá and Valencia; but the death of his father made it necessary for him to return home to carry on the family business. But though in the world, he was not of it, joining in all the services of the Church as far as his secular affairs permitted. He married, but lost both wife and a daughter in death not many years later. He and a little son then went to live with his mother and sister, both for economy's sake and for mutual consolation. Alphonsus dedicated his last surviving child to God, and he used daily to pray that the boy might be taken young rather than live to commit sin: the little boy died shortly after his fourth birthday.

His father then applied to be admitted into the Society of Jesus. As his studies had been curtailed, he was advised by Fr. Louis Santander to study Latin further so as to qualify himself for the course for the priesthood. Eventually, through the medium of Fr. Anthony Cordeses, Provincial of Aragon, he was accepted as a lay-brother. 'I think', said Fr. Cordeses, 'he will be useful to us all by his example and prayers.' He entered the noviciate at Valencia, 31st July, 1571, and after six months was transferred to the newly-opened College of Montesion at Majorca, where he took the solemn vows, 5th April, 1585.

For nearly fifty years, Alphonsus filled the obscure, but really very important position of hall-porter at the College with great exactness, offering up the almost innumerable irritations and vexations associated with that daily routine, as so many acts of mortification. Though not learned as the result of study, he soon became filled with that infused knowledge, instances of which are so often seen in the lives of the saints, and at the Sunday Conferences at the College on moral and speculative questions, the opinion of the holy lay-brother was looked forward to by theologians, canonists, and civil lawyers as that of an inspired oracle. His advice was sought by numbers of persons both religious and lay, and among these by Fr. Peter Claver, the Apostle of the Negroes, who was a student at the College during a part of this time. St. Alphonsus foretold that the young philosopher would one day go to the Indies—as America was then often termed—and there win many souls to God! He foretold the day of his death and having received the last rites with his wonted fervour, 'el Santo', as he was already called by the people of the place, passed to his reward on 31st October, 1617.

Crowds of persons came to venerate the remains of one who had for years been looked up to as an example of extraordinary sanctity. His obsequies were attended by the Viceroy, the notables of the town and representatives of all the religious orders, and such was the popular demand for relics of the deceased, that two Dominican monks, we are told, were kept busy touching the coffin with the medals that were handed to them in bunches by the people! The body of the wonderful lay-brother rests in a vault of the Lady Chapel of the Cathedral of Majorca. He was canonized by Leo XIII, 6th September, 1887. Many miracles, cures of malignant and troublesome diseases chiefly, have been ascribed to the intercession of the saint, who also left behind him several MS. volumes of notes and reflections on various spiritual subjects, all remarkable for sound doctrine and intense devotion.

The first letter was written in Majorca on 23rd April, 1609, and the second, to a novice, on 12th March, 1593.

St. Charles Borromeo

1538–1584

Reverend fathers,

        I have no need to describe to you the miserable state of this city [Milan] since it is open to the eyes of all, nor to rouse you to compassion, for no one can be so hard-hearted as not to feel for the afflicted. Yet this I will say, that it is no ordinary calamity which we have now to endure. We see men in the hour of their need deprived of the presence and support of those nearest and dearest to them. We see them torn from their abodes and dragged to a place of suffering, which is more like a stable than a hospital, and this with little or no hope of again beholding their relatives or homes. This would be grievous indeed even if it only concerned the frail bodies which must one day perish, though there would then be this consolation, that they would soon be rewarded for their pains by an eternity of joy. But here it is worse than this: it is not their bodies alone which are in danger of perishing, it is their souls, for which I plead. Though reduced to a condition so desperate, they have none to minister to their needs in spiritual things. Shall we not be heartless indeed if we stand by and stretch out no hands to help? Shall we see our brethren and fellow-citizens, our friends and relatives, not only deprived of comforts in their sufferings, not only tortured with pain and the apprehension of a terrible death: but shall we stand idly by and see them without any of the consolations of religion, while they call on us with tears to take pity on them, while their very looks tell us, when they have lost their voices, that their days are without help and their end almost without hope? Shall these things take place before our eyes, and we give no relief? O reverend fathers, here is your opportunity to prove your title to the name of religious, to effect all your good desires and resolutions, to serve God by acts of heroic perfection. This is the time to show forth the excellence of your institute, that you are striving to be saints and to lead perfect lives, for it is chiefly by works of piety and mercy that perfection is to be shown. O turn not your backs upon an occasion of serving God in a way so charitable and so necessary, reject not the prayers of these wretched suppliants. It is a work that falls more clearly to your share, for the city clergy have their hands full in a season of such distress. We know that they are faithful in performing their ordinary duties, and that they could not suffice for more than this even if they were in greater numbers than they are. But besides this, if they were to mingle with the plague-stricken, they would be shunned as bearers of contagion among their own people, so that we should have to provide other clergy for parochial duties. We have exerted ourselves to procure the services of priests from the country, and some have offered themselves, but they do not suffice for all that is required of them, and there are numbers of patients in the huts beyond the walls who are altogether without the ministrations of the Church, because we have no priests to send to them.

It is to you then we look in this emergency, to you who, living in a state of perfection, are obliged by your profession to make no account of temporal considerations, but to despise them, whenever you may thereby serve God more perfectly. To you we look, who ought to be ready to lay down your lives for the love of God and your neighbour, especially when it is a question of saving souls. For it was thus that the Son of God died for us, and thus many saints

167

have done, whose example you as good religious are bound to follow.

But you will say, perhaps, that in the case of the sick, whose cause we are pleading, your good offices are not so essential, seeing they may be saved without you. We do not now dispute the point, nor will we consider the matter on a ground so low. The holy law of the Gospel, and the example of the saints, teach us to exercise generosity. The saints knew no law but that of charity, and never shrank from devoting themselves to such works as this which we now propose to you. Jesus Christ our Lord in His own person bears out the lesson. Though the Son of God, He gave Himself of His own will to a death of shame upon the cross, for friends and for enemies.

It is He who invites you to take part in the work. Though we have spoken of the duty of not counting our lives dear to us in His cause, we do not wish you to understand that there is of necessity danger to health or life. By God's grace it is far otherwise, and with ordinary caution and attention to rules, risk may be avoided, as is done by those priests who have hitherto laboured here. But this we say, that if it should please Almighty God that any of us should catch the infection and die, that it would be a glorious end, rather deserving the name of life, for dying thus in the service of God and of our neighbours, it is most certain that we should attain to life eternal—that life which the saints and martyrs have made the end and aim of their labours upon earth.

Moreover, it is an opportunity of showing our gratitude to God, and laying up a treasure of merit for ourselves, making a generous return for the love which the Son of God has lavished upon us, offering up our lives in His service and in that of His plague-stricken brethren, even as He laid down His life for us on the cross, nay, even as He gives

168

it to us His priests every day in the Holy Sacrifice of the Mass.

Who is there among you whose heart is so cold as not to respond to the call of our dear Lord, to whom we are so bound? Who can refrain from offering himself, his health and life, and all that he has, in sacrifice to Him? Shall we suffer ourselves to be overcome by the fear of death? In any case we must die ere long. What security have we, again, that if we abandon our duty in keeping out of the reach of pestilence, that the just judgement of God will not overtake us, and thus punish our inordinate affection for our perishing bodies? Believe me, reverend fathers, it is an easy thing to fall a victim to this common visitation. We have innumerable examples before us of those who have hedged themselves round with every possible precaution, but have nevertheless perished. For it is a scourge sent by God for the chastisement of our sins, and who shall deliver us from the hand of His power when it is His will to search us out?

Far better for us, therefore, would it be to abandon ourselves to God by entering upon this holy work for love of Him, and in satisfaction for our sins—thus, so to speak, restraining His arm, and calling upon His mercy.

Dear fathers, what shall I say more? Shall I reproach you with the example of laymen, who, for a little temporal gain, expose themselves to far greater danger in their attendance than is required of us—touching them, handling them, and waiting upon them in every way? But I will go further, and say there are many of them who do this, not for fee or reward, but from pure love of God. This we know of ourselves, for many have placed their services freely at our disposal. And shall *we* do less, His priests, who are the recipients of His special favours, who make profession of leading a spiritual and perfect life? Shall we suffer ourselves to be outstripped by people in the world? shall not the love of God have greater weight with us than mere interest and gain has with them? Have we not indeed our own true interest at heart? Is not the reward of glory which God will render us in His eternal kingdom more to us than perishing gain is to them? Think of these things, beloved brethren and fathers and show not yourselves to be so weak and faint-hearted that laymen shall rise up in judgement against you and condemn you.

If any of you are withheld from offering yourselves by reason of not having the permission of your superiors, though we will not believe that the charity of any superior is so weak that he would not wish to second your good desires, know that the Sovereign Pontiff hereby releases you from all obligation of obedience on this occasion: and we have received ample faculties from His Holiness to authorize you to come even against the express will of your superiors. Let not this therefore distress you. Far from incurring any guilt of disobedience, you will be doing what is most pleasing to His Holiness, to which he himself exhorts and invites you.

I call upon you one and all therefore to devote yourselves generously to this work worthy of your high calling, and to make your service a special oblation to Almighty God, who has vouchsafed to charge Himself with the reward of all you do for Him. Moreover, I ask it of you as a favour personal to myself, of which I shall never be unmindful. For I assure you, you will hereby relieve me of a burden which oppresses me beyond measure, and I shall be greatly rejoiced when I see you occupied in saving these souls committed to my charge, and so dear to me, that I may say I bear them graven on my heart. You may imagine the grief and anguish I feel to see them in danger of perishing eternally for want of spiritual assistance. I do not doubt, however, that you will readily offer yourselves that I may send you out to them, or that the example of the first-comers will inspire many others to do likewise. When the work is once begun, God, I know, will move many hearts to carry it on. But as the risk of those who are first to offer themselves is greater, let them rest assured that their reward shall be higher. Fear not, my brethren, ever to be forsaken under any circumstances that may arise; I myself will keep my eye upon you, and will never forsake you. If it should please God that any of you fall a prey to the disease, and there should be none to serve you, I will attend you myself and have every care for your souls. For my own part, you are my witnesses, that from this hour I devote myself to minister to you in holy things. I am firmly resolved that no weariness, no fatigue, no peril, shall make me quail from fulfilling my pastoral office, or from doing everything in my power for the souls which God has committed to my keeping.

CHARLES BORROMEO, the son of the Count Arona of Milan, was born 2nd October, 1538, at Arona on Lake Maggiore, and died 4th November, 1584, in Milan. His uncle, Pope Pius IV, called him in 1560 to Rome, named him cardinal, conferred on him the archbishopric of Milan and made him papal secretary of state. The Cardinal was responsible for the reopening and the closing of the Council of Trent (18th January, 1562–3rd December, 1563), the carrying out of its decrees in the curia, and the drawing up of the *Catechismus Romanus*. From Pius V, whose election he had super-vised, he obtained permission to leave Rome and to devote himself to the reform of his ecclesiastical province of Milan. Through numberless provincial and diocesan synods, through endless visita-tions and countless pastoral conferences, through his concern for the education of an able clergy and for the discipline of the monastic orders, the ecclesiastical life of this region took on fresh impetus. His legislative work at the synods made him, in the expression of

Bishop Valiers of Verona, 'the teacher of bishops'. For what had been established as groundwork by the Council of Trent, was in Borromeo's subsequent legislation elaborated to the smallest detail, with a universally admired understanding for the necessary and the feasible. From everywhere bishops requested copies of the decisions of his first provincial council, and soon these were distributed throughout Christendom. Enlarged by many later episcopal letters and ordinances, these *Acta Ecclesiae Mediolanensis* saw many editions. In the bull of Borromeo's canonization, Pope Paul V mentions explicitly that they are used constantly by the bishops and constitute an abundant treasure of instruction in the government of the Church.

As reformer also, Borromeo constantly referred himself to the decisions of the Council of Trent, and where these did not suffice, he based them on the Church fathers and the decisions of earlier councils. It is this constant union with tradition which gives his work its strength and lasting influence. In the sixteenth century, renovation had to be carried on even in the ecclesiastical domain, and as reformer Borromeo did not escape misinterpretation and misuse of his words. The Council of Trent had based the renovation of the Church on the episcopal authority and laid it in the hands of the bishops. It was therefore of first importance that the Cardinal of Milan set an example as to how the decisions of the council were to be put into practice and as to what could be attained by their judicious application. What had fallen into disuse now became re-invigorated. It can truly be said that Borromeo's work as bishop extended to the whole Catholic Church, as is proved by a correspondence which fills 300 volumes, stored to this day in the Biblioteca Ambrosiana. A full appreciation of the measure of his arduous labours must surely excite boundless admiration: for this correspondence was only a by-product in an otherwise extremely busy life filled with daily audiences, visits, numerous sermons and public addresses, visitations of his own bishopric and of other dioceses, preparations for seventeen councils.

To his contemporaries, his name spelt reform. He yielded to no other Church reformer in courage, endurance, intrepidity, and sheer ardour of work. What stands foremost in him is the complete self-effacement in his devotion to his task. Already as a young student in Pavia he resisted all the temptations of a gay university town. And once raised to the cardinalate, this austerity only increased. As archbishop he finally knew only one goal; to let his own self die, so as to live more fully in his great task. His only relaxation now was prayer, in which he spent as many hours as he could spare, sacrificing, however, even this joy at the slightest call of his episcopal duties. The austerity of his life in fasting and denial of sleep approached that of the anchorites; many even thought that he went too far in these mortifications. For the reformer Borromeo, however, this austerity proved a valuable help in the difficulties of his life and office: it made manifest to all that the Archbishop had renounced every worldly ambition and coveted nothing for himself.

With the exception of the founder of the Jesuits, no one has influenced the Catholic renaissance so deeply and lastingly as the towering personality of Charles. To Borromeo the high office he held was a gift of God to be used only for His honour. His years were short but full, crammed with all the hectic struggles of the false and the true reformations. From the clergy, laity, and particularly from a series of petty, proud governors appointed by Philip the Prudent of Spain, he met violent opposition. When the plague visited Milan in 1576, priests fled, the Governor fled, the rich fled, so Borromeo tended the sick and buried the dead with his own hands. He knew years of strife and also years of loving care for his flock. He literally worked himself to death.

He died in November, 1584, in the prime of life, but worn out by the extreme privation in which he thought it right to live. His remains were laid in a crystal shrine in the crypt under the dome of Milan Cathedral; his head was taken to Rome and rests under the altar of San Carlo al Corso, where there is a picture of the Virgin Mother presenting St. Charles to her Son. A crucifix which he carried in a procession is in a chapel of the Duomo at Milan, and some of his letters are to be seen in the Biblioteca.

A congregation of secular priests called the Oblates of St. Charles, have charge of some London parishes.

Bl. Edmund Campion

1540–1581

IT is not now as of old the dash of youth, or facility of pen, nor any punctilious care of regularity in correspondence, that makes me write to you. I used to write from the mere abundance of my heart: a greater necessity has forced me to write this letter. We have already been too long subservient to popular report, to the times, to reputation. At length let us say something for the salvation of our souls. I beg you, by your own natural goodness, by my tears, even by the pierced side of Christ and the wounds of the Crucified, to listen to me.

There is no end nor measure to my thinking of you; and I never think of you without being horribly ashamed, praying silently, and repeating the text of the Psalm, *Ab alienis, Domine, parce servo tuo.* 'From the sins of others, O Lord, spare Thy servant.' What have I done? It is written: *Videbas furem et currebas cum eo;* and *Laudatur peccator in desideriis suis, et impius benedicitur.* 'Thou didst see the thief, and didst run with him. The sinner is praised in his desires, and the impious is blest.'

So often was I with you at Gloucester, so often in your private chamber, so many hours have I spent in your study and library, with no one near us when I could have done this business, and I did it not; and what is worse, I have added flames to the fever by assenting and assisting. And though you were superior to me in your counterfeited dignity, in wealth, age, and learning; and although I was not bound to look after the physicking or dieting of your

174

soul, yet since you were of so easy and sweet a temper, as in spite of your grey hairs to admit me, young as I was, to a familiar intercourse with you, to say whatever I chose in all security and secrecy, while you imparted to me your sorrows and all the calumnies of the other heretics against you. Like a father, you exhorted me to walk straight and upright in the royal road, to follow the steps of the Church, the Councils and Fathers, and to believe that, where there was a consensus of these, there could be no stain of falsehood. This now makes me very angry with myself for my false modesty or culpable negligence, because I made no use of so fair an opportunity of recommending the Faith, and applied no bold incentive to one who was so near to the Kingdom of God, but, while I enjoyed your favour and renown, I promoted rather the shadowy notion of my own honour than your eternal good.

But as I have no longer the occasion that I had of persuading you face to face, it remains that I should send my words to you to witness to my regard, my care, my anxiety known to Him to whom I make my daily prayer for your salvation. Listen, I beseech you, listen to a few words. You are sixty years old more or less, of uncertain health, of weakened body, the hatred of heretics, the shame of Catholics, the talk of the people, the sorrow of your friends, the laughing-stock of your enemies. Against your conscience you falsely usurp the name of a bishop; by your silence you advance a pestilent sect which you love not, stricken with anathema, cut off from the body into which alone the graces of Christ flow, you are deprived of the benefit of all prayers, sacrifices, and sacraments. Whom do you think yourself to be? What do you expect? What is your life? Wherein lies your hope? Is it in the heretics, who hate you so implacably, and abuse you so roundly? Is it because of all heresiarchs you are the least crazy?

Because you confess the true presence of Christ on the altar and the freedom of man's will? Because you persecute no Catholics within your diocese? Because you are hospitable to your townspeople and to good men? Because you have not plundered your palace and lands as your brethren do?

Surely these things will avail much if you return to the bosom of the Church; if in company with the household of the faith you suffer even the smallest persecution; or take any wholesome counsel. But now whilst you are a stranger and an enemy, whilst like a base deserter you fight under a foreign flag, it is in vain to attempt to cover your many crimes with the cloak of virtue. You will gain nothing except perhaps to be tortured somewhat less horribly in the everlasting fire than Judas, or Luther, or Zwinglius, or than those antagonists of yours—Cooper, Humphrey, and Samson. What signifies the kind of death? Death is the same, whether you are thrown from a high rock into the sea or pushed from a low bank into the river; whether one is killed by iron or by rope, whether racked in torture or shot dead, whether cut down by sword or axe, whether crushed under stones or battered by clubs, whether roasted with fire or scalded in water.

What is the use of fighting for many articles of the Faith and to perish for doubting of a few? To escape shipwreck and to fall by the dagger? To flee from the plague and die of famine? To avoid the flames and be suffocated by the smoke? He believes no one article of the Faith who refuses to believe any single one. For as soon as he knowingly oversteps the bounds of the Church, which is the pillar and ground of the truth, to which Christ Jesus, the highest, first, and most simple truth, the source, light, leader, measure, and pattern of the faithful, reveals all these articles—however many Catholic dogmas he retains, yet if he perniciously plucks out one, that which he holds, he holds not by orthodox faith, without which it is impossible to please God, but by his own reason, his own conviction.

In vain do you defend the religion of the Catholics if you hug only that which you like, and cut off all that seems not right in your eyes. There is but one plain known road, not enclosed by your palings or mine, not by private judgement, but by the severe laws of humility and obedience; when you wander from this you are lost. You must be altogether within the house of God, within the walls of salvation, to be sound and safe from injury; if you wander and walk abroad ever so little, if you carelessly thrust hand or foot out of the ship, if you stir up ever so small a mutiny in the crew, you shall be thrust forth; the door is shut, the ocean roars, you are undone.

'He who gathereth not with Me,' saith the Saviour, 'scattereth.' Jerome explains, 'he who is not Christ's is Antichrist's.' You are not so stupid as to follow the heresy of the Sacramentarians; you are not so mad as to be in all things a slave of Luther's faction, now condemned in the General Councils, which you yourself think authoritative, of Constance and Trent. And yet you stick in the mire of your own conceit, so that you may pose as a man who brings to light the artifices of pedants, and who presides as an honoured judge over the poorer brethren.

You will remember the sober and solemn answer which you gave me, when three years ago we met in the house of Thomas Dutton, at Sherborne, where we were to dine. We fell to talking of St. Cyprian. I objected to you, in order to discover your real opinions, that synod of Carthage which erred about the baptism of infants. You answered truly that the Holy Spirit was not promised to one province, but to the Church; that the Universal Church is represented in a full Council, and that no doctrine can be pointed out about which such Councils ever erred. Acknowledge your weapons, with which you conquer the adversaries of the mystery of the Eucharist. You cry up the Christian world, the assemblies of bishops, the guardians of the deposit, that is, the ancient faith; these you commend to the people as the interpreters of Scripture; most rightly do you ridicule and hold up to scorn the impudent figment of certain professors of false patristic.

Now what do you say? Behold the renowned Fathers, the patriarchs and apostolic men, of late gathered at Trent, who were all united to contend for the ancient faith of the Fathers. Legates, prelates, cardinals, bishops, deputies, doctors of diverse nations, of mature age, of rare wisdom, princely dignity, wonderful learning. There were collected Italians, Frenchmen, Spaniards, Portuguese, Greeks, Poles, Hungarians, Flemings, Illyrians, many Germans, some Irish, Croats, Moravians—even England was not unrepresented. All these, whilst you live as you are living, anathematize you, drive you out, banish you, abjure you. What reason can you urge? Especially now you have declared war against your colleagues, why do you not make full submission, without any exceptions, to the discipline of these Fathers? See you aught in the Lord's Supper that they saw not, discussed not, resolved not? Dare you equal yourself by even the hundredth part with the lowest theologians of this Council? I have confidence in your discretion and modesty, you dare not. You are surpassed then by your judges in number, value, weight, and in the serious and clear testimony of the whole world.

Once more consult your own heart, my poor old friend. Show again your old nobility of character and those excellent gifts which of late are smothered in the mud of dishonesty. Give yourself to your mother who begot you to Christ, nourished you, consecrated you; acknowledge how cruel and undutiful you have been; let confession be the salve of your sins. You have one foot in the grave; you must die, perhaps directly, certainly in a very short time, and stand before that tribunal where you will hear, 'give an account of thy stewardship'. Unless, while you are on the way, you make it up quickly and exactly with the Adversary of sin, it shall be required to the last farthing, and you shall be driven miserably from the land of the living by Him Whom you will never be able to pay.

Then those hands which have conferred spurious Orders on so many wretched youths shall for very pain scratch and tear your sulphurous body; that mouth stained with perjury, and defiled with schism, shall be filled with fire and worms and the breath of tempests. That swelling carnal pomp of yours, your episcopal throne, your yearly revenues, spacious palace, honourable greetings, band of servants, elegant furniture, that affluence for which the poor ignorant people esteem you so happy, shall be exchanged for fearful wailings, gnashing of teeth, stench, misery, filth, and chains. There shall the spirits of Calvin and Zwingli, whom you now oppose, afflict you for ever, with Arius, Sabellius, Nestorius, Wyclif, Luther—yea, with the devil and his angels you shall suffer the pains of darkness and belch out blasphemies.

Spare yourself, be merciful to your soul, spare my grief, Your ship is wrecked, your merchandise lost; nevertheless seize the plank of penance, strike out with all your might, and come even naked to the harbour of the Church. Fear not but that Christ will preserve you with His hand, run to meet you, kiss you, and put on you the white garment; the hosts of Heaven will exult. Take no thought for your life; He will take thought for you, Who gives the beasts their food, and feeds the young ravens that call upon Him.

If you but made trial of our banishment, if you but cleared your conscience and came to behold and consider the living examples of piety which are shown here by bishops, priests, friars, masters of colleges, rulers of provinces, lay people of every age, rank and sex, I believe that you would give up six hundred Englands for the opportunity of redeeming the residue of your time by tears and sorrow. But if for divers reasons you are hindered from going freely whither you would, at least free your mind from its grievous chains, and whether you remain or whether you flee, set your body any task, rather than let its grossness oppress you, and banish you to the depths of Hell. God knows those that are His, and is near to all that call upon Him in truth.

Pardon, my venerated old friend, for these just reproaches and for the heat of my love. Suffer me to hate that deadly disease, let me avert the perilous crisis of so noble a man and so dear a friend, with any dose however bitter. That it will be so—if Christ gives grace and you do not refuse—I hope as firmly as I love you dearly, and I love you as passing excellent in nature, in learning, in gentleness, in goodness, and as doubly dear to me for your many kindnesses and courtesies. If you recover yourself, you make me happy for ever; if you decline, this letter is my witness. God judge between you and me, your blood be on yourself. Farewell. From him that most desires your salvation.

EDMUND CAMPION

AMONG the many good deeds of a famous foundation must be reckoned the scholarship at St. John's College, Oxford, which the Grocers' Company in 1556 gave to young Edmund Campion, son of a London bookseller—a brilliant boy with a 'future', who had already won much academic glory for his school, Christ's Hospital, by winning all kinds of scholastic laurels in open competition with the other London schools which then, we are told, formed a sort of junior university. Till the end of the eighteenth century brought Lamb and Coleridge on to the scene, no such meteoric 'Blue Coat boy' was to grace Edward VI's memorable foundation. Campion as the 'Captain' of the school, had in elegant Latin diction welcomed Queen Mary to the City (1553), as later he was to orate before her sister, Queen Elizabeth, at Oxford in a speech that might have come from Cicero. In August, 1569, Campion, 'full of remorse of conscience and detestation of mind', left Oxford.

With enemies all round him, 'our good Edmund' made for Douai, where at last he was to find rest of soul. There he was 're-ceived', and at the University took his long sought for B.D. In the character of Campion there was always something of the soldier, and it is not surprising, therefore, that by 1573, the momentous convert should have been enlisted in the Society of Jesus.

The Jesuits were not unduly eager to undertake the terribly perilous work then to be done in England. Possibly they considered that their advent would embitter the persecution and worsen the lot of the Catholics. The coming of seminary priests from Douai on the English mission had already led to an ominous change in the direction of greater severity on the part of the Burleigh-Walsing-ham administration. Towards the end of April, 1580, Campion, Fr. Parsons, and a lay-brother named Ralph Emerson, left for England after receiving the blessing of the Pope, Gregory XIII, who liked Englishmen, but not their Queen. Dr. Goldwell, Bishop of St. Asaph, was also of the party, but age, illness, and the Pope's command soon made it expedient for the last of the ancient hier-archy to turn back at Rheims.

Separating for safety's sake, Parsons, disguised as a Captain, got to Dover first, and with the utmost self-possession requested the offi-cials there to show all courtesy to a friend of his, a 'jewel merchant', who would arrive very shortly! The 'jewel merchant'—Campion of course—and the 'Captain' were in London in a few days. The arrival of the Jesuits alarmed others than the Government. So fearful were the Catholics in and about London of the probable conse-quences, that a secret meeting was held in Southwark that July to request the newcomers to state their intentions.

For months the sleuths of the law were completely baffled, and meanwhile the Campion furore passed like a flame from London to Yorkshire and Lancashire. Not only Catholics, but Protestants came in ever-increasing numbers to the secret chapels and meeting-places to hear the illustrious Jesuit discourse. He made men and women feel—many, perhaps, for the first time—that eternity is the only thing that really matters! His sermons were brilliant in style and replete with learning, yet without the curse of dryness that mere pedantry often brings.

On 27th June, 1581, 400 copies of the famous and secretly printed *Decem Rationes*, were scattered about the benches of St. Mary's, Oxford, the day of the 'Commemoration', and before long hundreds, perhaps thousands, were reading a book which was to pass through edition after edition at home and abroad, and to mark an epoch in religious controversy. It was Campion's last lightning stroke, however, as a free man. On 6th July, sixty Catholics assembled at Lyford Grange, Berkshire, to hear him preach. The owner, Mrs. Yates, gave hospitality to some dispossessed Bridgettine nuns there, but one of Leicester's spies, the apostate, George Eliot, got news of the Mass and sermon at the Grange, and very soon the place was surrounded.

The original charge, that of attaching people to the Church of Rome, was dropped so as to rob the trial of all appearance of persecution! Campion, though weak from his rackings, had little difficulty in disposing of the perjured evidence of such 'witnesses' as Eliot, Sledd and Munday, and in showing the monstrous absurdity of the 'conspiracy' accusation. The jury, though carefully picked, were evidently impressed by the excellent defence, for they were an hour deliberating before coming to their verdict of guilty. He was martyred on 1st December, 1581.

St. John of the Cross
1542–1591

YOU have seen, daughter, what a good thing it is to be without money, for, if we have any, people can rob us of it, and disturb our quiet, and also how the treasures of the soul should be hidden away and left in peace, so that we may not know they are there, or even so much as catch a glimpse of them; for there is no worse thief than one who lives in the house. May God preserve us from ourselves; may He give us whatever pleases Him and never reveal it to us until it be His will to do so. After all, he who lays up treasures for love's sake lays them up for another, and it is well that He should keep them for Himself and enjoy them, since they are all for Him, and that we ourselves should neither see them with our eyes nor enjoy them, lest we should rob God of the pleasure which He has in the humility and detachment of our hearts and our contempt of worldly things for His sake. It is a very great treasure, and one that brings great joy, for the soul to discover that it is going to give Him such manifest pleasure, and to pay no heed to the foolish ones of this world, who can keep nothing for the future.

The Masses will be said, and I shall be very glad to go if they do not advise me to the contrary. May God keep you.

FRAY JOHN OF THE CROSS

*

JESUS. MARY.

In these days be employed inwardly in desiring the coming of the Holy Spirit, and both during the festival and afterwards continue in His presence, and let your care and esteem for this be such that nothing else attracts you, neither consider aught else, whether it be trouble or any other disturbing memories; and during the whole of this period, even though there be omissions in the house, pass them over for the love of the Holy Spirit, and for the sake of what is necessary to the peace and quiet of the soul wherein He loves to dwell.

If you can put an end to your scruples, I think it would be better for your quietness if you were not to confess during these days. When you do confess, let it be after this manner: with regard to advertences and thoughts, whether they have respect to judgements or whether to unruly representations of objects or any other movements that come to you without the desire and collaboration of your soul, and without your desiring to pay attention to them, do not confess these or take any notice of them or be anxious about them, for it is better to forget them, although they trouble your soul the more; at most you might describe in general terms the omission or remissness that you may perchance have noted with respect to the purity and perfection which you should have in the interior faculties— memory, understanding and will. With respect to words, confess such excess and lack of modesty as you may have committed in speaking truly and uprightly, of necessity and with purity of intention. With regard to actions, confess the way in which you may have diverged from the path to your true and only goal, which you should follow without respect of persons—namely, God alone.

And, if you confess in this way, you may rest content,

without confessing any of these other things in particular, however much interior conflict it may bring you. You will communicate during this festival, within the customary period.

When anything disagreeable and displeasing happens to you, remember Christ crucified and be silent.

Live in faith and hope, though it be in darkness, for in this darkness God protects the soul. Cast your care upon God for you are His and He will not forget you. Think not that He leaves you alone, for this would be to wrong Him.

Read, pray, rejoice in God, your Good and your Health, and may He give you His good things and preserve you wholly, even to the day of eternity. Amen. Amen.

FRAY JOHN OF THE CROSS

*

JESUS be in Your Reverence. Think not, daughter in Christ, that I have ceased to grieve for you in your trials or for those that share them with you; yet, when I remember that God has called you to lead an apostolic life, which is a life of contempt, and in leading you by that road, I am comforted. Briefly, God desires that the religious shall live the religious life in such a way that he shall have done with everything, and everything shall be as nothing to him. For He Himself desires to be the only wealth of the soul and its comfort and its delectable glory. A surpassing favour has God granted Your Reverence, for now, forgetting all things, Your Reverence will be able to rejoice in God alone, and for love of God will care nothing as to what they do with you, since you belong not to yourself but to God.

Let me know if your departure for Madrid is certain, and if the Mother Prioress is coming, and commend me greatly to my daughters Magdalena and Ana, and to them all, for I have no opportunity to write to them.

From Granada, on the 8th of February, [15]88.

FRAY JOHN OF THE CROSS

*

HOW long, daughter, do you suppose that you will be carried in the arms of others? I desire to see in you so great a detachment from the creatures and an independence of them that hell itself would not suffice to trouble you. What are these uncalled-for tears that you are shedding nowadays? How much good time do you suppose you have wasted on these scruples? If you would communicate your trials to me, go to that spotless mirror of the Eternal Father, which is His Son, for in that mirror I behold your soul daily, and I doubt not but that you will come away from it comforted and will have no need to go begging at the doors of poor people.

*

JESUS be in your soul, my daughter in Christ. Your letter filled me with pity for your trouble and I grieve that you have it because of the harm that it may cause your spirit and even your bodily health. Know then that it seems not to me that you have such cause to feel this grief as you do, since I do not . . . to our Father . . . with no kind of misfortune . . . remembrance of such . . . and even if there were . . . it will be . . . your repentance; and if there

were still any [trouble] . . . I . . . given . . . to speak well.
Be not troubled about it and take no account of it, for there
is no need. For I am certain that it is a temptation which the
devil brings to the spirit so that it may occupy in it that
which should be occupied in God. Have courage, my
daughter, and be given greatly to prayer, forgetting this
and that, for after all we have no other blessing nor . . .
support, nor comfort (than?) this, and after we have left
all for God it is right that we should have no support
or comfort in aught save Him. And yet it is a great . . .
for us to have Him, so that He may (stay?) with us
and that He may give nothing . . . for the soul that . . .
comfort and thinking that . . . His Majesty will be . . .
when we are not in trouble, for . . . is not . . . I will do
it.

BORN at Fontibere, in Old Castile, John entered the Carmelite
Order when twenty-one years of age. He underwent considerable
self-mortification and determined to join the more austere Carthu-
sians; but after he had met St. Teresa of Avila, she persuaded him to
enter one of her reformed Carmelite houses for men. He did so at
Durvello, until the monastery was moved to Mancera. In 1570
John was put in charge of the house of the Order at Pastrana, and
the next year at Alcalá. He founded a house at Breza in 1579, and
was made Vicar-Provincial in Andalusia in 1585. This bare-footed
monk was not loved for his severity, and the reformed Order
rebelled; he was dismissed from his office and imprisoned at Ubeda,
where he died. St. John wrote some of the greatest poetry, and St.
Teresa says that he was one of the purest souls in the Church. His
relics are at Segovia. His mystical treatises are of the utmost value
and his poems perfect gems. Roy Campbell has made a very fine
translation of them.

As in the case of his contemporary, Teresa of Avila, we give here
only a few letters, because his correspondence is so well known.
The second letter was addressed to a Carmelite nun who suffered

from scruples, the third to Leonor Bautista at Beas, the fourth to the Prioress of Caravaca, and the fifth to Leonor de San Gabriel at Córdoba. The original letters may be seen at San Lúcar la Mayor. He was canonized in 1726, and declared a Doctor of the Church in 1926.

St. Robert Bellarmine

1542–1621

THIS is a great evil, because it teaches the boys to be sneaks and cowards, as St. Paul warns us, and because they get accustomed to tell lies in order to escape being beaten. Besides, the children of gentlemen ought to be led on by honourable inducements and not by fear of being flogged. I myself was a master when young in our Society, and I never inflicted corporal punishment on a single boy, nor advised others to do so. By emulation and a threat now and again, I got them on far better than some of my colleagues did, who thrashed them. St. Augustine, who also kept a school in his time, severely rebukes in his Confessions the tyranny of masters in venting their cruelty on poor little children.

★

VERY Reverend and Most Learned Sir,
Your letter afforded me immense joy. I thanked God with all my heart for the singular grace which He has given you. It is granted to few to recognize the true Church amid the darkness of so many schisms and heresies, and to still fewer so to love the truth which they have seen as to fly to its embrace, generously despising comfort, honour and, above all, royal favour, the unfailing source of such earthly prizes. If in your voluntary exile you have to endure sorrow and want for Our Lord's sake, you will be blessed indeed, being made worthy not only to believe

in Christ with your whole heart, but also to suffer for His Name. As in Heaven nothing will be sweeter than to resemble Him in His glory, so here on earth nothing is more to our advantage than to be like Him in His Passion. Hence arises that solid and perennial joy which nobody can steal from us. . . . I do not write this in any spirit of indifference to your present need, which I am more than willing to assist as far as I can, but because I congratulate you from my heart not only on account of your reception into the Church, outside which there is no salvation, but also for the precious gift of patience with which I think Our Lord has adorned your soul. As for my part in the matter, you owe me no thanks at all, for 'neither he who plants is anything, nor he who waters, but God it is who gives the increase'. I only pass on to others what our Catholic Mother has herself passed on to me. If there is any lack of learning in my writings, any obscurity of expression or superficial treatment, you may feel sure that it is in such places I am most original. And so farewell, most learned and worthy Sir. Remember me in your holy prayers.

CARDINAL BELLARMINE

★

YOUR affection for me makes you admire and think important anything that comes from my pen. But as a matter of fact, these notes on the *Summa* of St. Thomas are imperfect, incomplete, and to my mind, not worth publishing. They are imperfect because they do not contain all that I said when lecturing, being only a résumé. They are incomplete because there are two lacunae, one at the beginning of the *Prima Secundae*, and another and larger one at the end of Part III. Finally, they are not worth publishing because they are the notes of a young man who had not only to teach a class, but also to preach to the people, offices which singly would have been work enough for an individual. What you said in your letter made me afraid that some good men might want, in spite of me, to have the notes printed and published. I therefore sought out the Holy Father, and asked authorization to write in his name to the Apostolic Nuncio at Cologne, instructing him to forbid all the printers of that city, under pain of excommunication, to put these commentaries on the *Summa* in print, unknown to me and without my permission. And would you, my very loving brother, oblige me by taking the enclosed letter to his Reverence, the Nuncio.

ROBERT BELLARMINE was born at Montepulciano, Italy, and entered the Society of Jesus at the age of eighteen. He had a distinguished career, teaching theology at Louvain, teaching and preaching in Rome, working on the Vulgate Bible, and as rector of the Roman College. In 1598 he was made a cardinal. For three years he occupied the archbishopric of Capua and gave up all other activities to look after his flock. He then became head of the Vatican Library and took a prominent part in all the affairs of the Holy See. Among other controversies he answered King James I of England and the Scottish jurist Barclay. St. Robert was one of the greatest polemical theologians the Church has ever produced and her foremost teacher against the doctrines of the Reformers; his best-known writings are the four volumes of *Disputations,* his catechism of Christian doctrine, and the devotional works of his later years. He was canonized in 1930, and his body rests in the church of St. Ignazio in Rome.

The first letter was written to his brother Thomas in 1611. The second was addressed to Benjamin Antony Carica, Canon of Canterbury and Chaplain to King James I, recently received into the Catholic Church, and is dated 14th February, 1614. The last letter is to a converted Calvinist, Peter Gudsem.

Bl. John Juvenal Ancina

1545-1604

Most Rev. and Honoured Father,

I think your Reverence must still remember Vachedani, who was formerly your penitent at San Giovanni de' Fiorentini. He seems to me to be a deserving subject, and worthy of the grace which he seeks, of being admitted into our Congregation. Hence I enclose all the letters he has written me about this affair, that you may see the progress of it, and decide how it shall end. I will write also to the two Anchorites, who are staying at the vineyard. But for the rest I shall seek a more convenient time, as I am trying not to fatigue myself too much by writing many letters in this excessive heat, nor sermons (*a quibus scribendis jampridem omnino destiti*), nor anything else, especially as I have today just begun to look over the new quires of the Annals of Father Cesare, which I have great pleasure in doing, and very little trouble in scratching out, as, thanks be to God, and to the carefulness with which they have been sent to me, they are, without comparison, more correct than the two preceding volumes. Tell that holy man that he may expect to reap great fruit from his labours. Well done, well done, Father Cesare! *Aut Cæsar aut nihil.* A few days ago I heard from another Father Cesare, a Jesuit, that in their college here in Naples they are having the aforesaid Annals read in the refectory, and that they are held in great esteem by all. *Benedictus Dominus.* And a few months ago, I heard that they were highly prized by Fr. Mario d' Andria, a famous Dominican, and their chief casuist, and are even quoted in the pulpit, *in tractatu de Passione Domini. Non nobis, Domine, non nobis, sed nomini tuo da gloriam.*

The new work of Father Thomas the Rector gives us pleasant, substantial, and wholesome pasture in the refectory in the mornings, and in the evening the Annals, which all like, and which I hope will prove most useful and acceptable, not only to faithful Catholics, but also to our very adversaries and mortal enemies. The only thing I would wish is that there were more copious marginal notes, and greater vigilance in correcting the press; as has, I see, been used in the last sheets sent me. As to the former ones, *macte animo et virtute pater; sic itur ad astra.*

Father Camillus is making the epitome of the Annals manfully. *Itaque omnes in vinea Domini strenue collaborant.* I alone, weaker and more slothful, am living at ease and enjoying myself, reaping the fruits of the labours of others, like a boy with sweatmeats, or a drone in a hive. For in this is the saying true: that it is one man that soweth, and another that reapeth. Others have laboured and we have entered into their labours. Hence my confusion is greatly increased in that, being so worthless, useless, and inexperienced, and moreover not a little ignorant and presumptuous (*Coram Domino quia non mentior*), nevertheless, last week it fell to me to be made one of the assistants of our Father Rector: I leave your Reverence to imagine what a fine appearance I shall make as assistant or counsellor. *Dignum patella operculum, et nos quoque poma natamus. Nos numerus vulgi, et fruges consumere nati.* I am sure, when this is known, there will be many a fine peal of laughter. Father Bordi and Father Baronio together on one side, and Fathers Germanico and Gallo on the other, will laugh in the town, and most justly; but still, I console myself a little that others, such as Fathers Alessandro, Angelo,

Nicolò, Giulio, and Flaminio, as more compassionate, will take pity on me, and so will our Giovan Matteo, *jure fraternitatis*. In this great confusion and need therefore, besides my many other ordinary wants, I beg from all the help of their fervent prayers, and in fine from your Reverence, your holy and ample benediction.—Of your Rev. Paternity, unworthy son in Christ, and useless servant.

GIOVENALE ANCINA

HE was born at Fossano near Turin on 19th October, 1545. Although a pious boy, in early life he desired a secular career. He studied philosophy and medicine at Montpellier and Mendovi, and after his father's death went to the University of Pavia; he was a clever student, and at the age of twenty-four took a brilliant doctorate in both subjects. During the next few years he led an austere life and one of persistent prayer. Juvenal arrived in Rome for the Year of Jubilee 1575, and soon became acquainted with Philip Neri who induced him to join his Oratory and receive minor orders. After five years he was ordained priest and lived for many years in Naples, tormented with the desire for the cloistered life, before returning to the Roman Oratory. In 1602 the Duke of Savoy asked Clement VIII to fill two vacant sees in his territory and the Pope personally charged Bl. Juvenal to accept the see of Saluzzo. A few years later he was poisoned there and died on 31st August. His cause was introduced in 1624, and was not finally achieved until the nineteenth century.

The above letter, written from Naples in 1590, was addressed to St. Philip.

Ven. Anne of Jesus

1545–1621

I WOULD have come to see you, if I had not thought that I should have been in the way while you have so many invalids. I do not know why Our Lord wants to give the house such a bad reputation, unless it is that He wishes to mortify us all.

★

IT would be a much greater consolation to speak to your Reverence than to write, for I cannot say all I wish, nor what the sequel is to the devotion I have had all my life to Holy Job. It is impossible to understand properly the difference there is between desiring to suffer and actual suffering. Job complained that God showed His power by pursuing a dry straw. I am so completely reduced to this, my dear Father, that I cannot express it. In fact it is impossible to explain the state in which God keeps me. I used to call Him 'The Concealer of my sins', but just at present I can say that He is making them known by the chastisement He is applying to them—a chastisement so lamentable, and which makes me so restless, that I hide myself from those around me. Day and night my limbs are trembling. I get not an instant's repose. Nevertheless I am allowed to hear Mass every day and receive His Divine Majesty. For this they carry me to the little grate. There the trembling is so great, that it seems as if my very bones would be dislocated. . . .

★

EVERY day I am in greater need of God's help, and of that of His servants. I am very pleased that our dear good Father Master Antolinez has compassion on me; if he could see me I am quite sure he would be more sorry for me than Job's friends were for him, for Job, at least, could clean his sores with a potsherd, while I am unable to move hand and foot. . . .

★

SEE to what a state your poor mother is reduced, for she cannot even raise her hand to bless you. It is three years since I made the sign of the Cross. I can only bless you from my heart.

★

AT present, my Lord, all I can do is to endure these trials and excessive sufferings. It is a marvel that I am alive at all. For four years I have not been able to lie down even for an hour, and I only sleep for a few minutes at a time. I can only get about by dragging myself along the floor like a serpent; and in spite of the severe frost, I am consumed with such burning heat that I can scarcely bear the weight of my habit.

ANA LOBERA, more commonly known as Venerable Anne of Jesus, was a Carmelite nun and companion of St. Teresa. She was born in Old Castile, 1545, and died in Brussels 4th March, 1621. Left an orphan at an early age she went to live with her father's relatives, and in 1570 took the habit in St. Teresa's convent. Fifteen years later, with the help of St. John of the Cross, she made a foundation in Madrid. Her life was full of misunderstandings, both the Pope and Philip II being appealed to during various vicissitudes, and for a time she was deprived of daily Holy Communion. In 1604 she was in Paris and thenceforth made more foundations in Flanders and Poland. She remained prioress of Brussels to her death.

The second letter was written to Father Diego de Guevara in 1615, the third in 1616. The fourth extract is from a letter to Salamanca, dictated in November, 1616. The last letter was to her cousin, then Bishop of Badajos, in October, 1617.

St. Stanislaus Kostka

1550–1568

MY very good Lord and Friend,

My best wishes to you. Thanks be to God and to the intercession of the Virgin Mother of God, I have got half-way safe and sound. Jesus and my Virgin Mother have given me plenty of crosses on the road. Close to Vienna two of my servants (*aulici mei*) overtook me. As soon as I recognized them, I hid myself in a wood hard by, and thus escaped their onset. After climbing a number of hills, and passing through many a wood, when I was refreshing my wearied body with some bread by the side of a clear stream, I heard the tramp of a horse. I got up and looked at the rider. It was Paul! His steed was covered with foam, and his face was hotter than the sun. You can fancy, Ernest, how frightened I was.

All chance of flight was gone because of the rate at which he was riding. So I stood still. And plucking up courage, I went to the horseman, and just like a pilgrim begged respectfully for an alms. He asked about his brother, described his dress and his height to me, and said he was very like myself in appearance. I replied that in the early morning he had gone along this road. Without waiting a moment he put spurs to his horse, threw me some money, and went off at a gallop. As soon as I had thanked the Most Holy Virgin, my Mother Mary, I betook myself to a cave nearby to avoid being pursued. After staying there a short time, I resumed my journey.

Let me tell you another misfortune and of what crosses

Jesus my Lord made me a present, and learn from this to join me in praising Him. My brother had paid the guards at the gates of the towns and villages to look out for his runaway Stanislaus, to cross-question and examine him, and he had given them a full description of me. This was a great trouble to me, but I chanced to meet one of the Society of Jesus, who was on his way, by order of his superiors, from Vienna to Dillingen. He recognized me, and I told him the reason of my journey, of my disguise, and of my brother's pursuit, and I explained to him the difficulties I had to encounter at the gates of the various towns. Accordingly to evade the two first posts he took me in a carriage. He would have driven me the whole way to Dillingen, if my desire to be unknown and to suffer for my Jesus had not stood in the way.

At length, after going through so many troubles, I reached Dillingen, where I was most kindly received by the Fathers of the Society, and was presented to the Reverend Father Provincial, from whom I received the favour I so much desired of being accepted. O Ernest, if you knew how happy I am! I find a heaven in the midst of saucepans and brooms. I beg you when you get this letter to pray that my Jesus may deign to show His love to me by manifold crosses and afflictions, and to keep me as His sinful little servant among His holy ones. And may you, Ernest, be faithful to your holy vocation. I shall not forget you *ad lumina apostolorum*.

ST. STANISLAUS KOSTKA is the example for all novices. He was descended from the Polish nobility and was born at the Castle of Rostkow, Poland. When he was fourteen years old, he was sent with an elder brother to the Jesuit College in Vienna. The perfect simplicity of his character, joined with his unchangeable cheerfulness and affability, made him a universal favourite; and the ardour with which he gave himself up to prayer, and the eloquence and unction with which he spoke to his companions of his purity, and the joy of perfect obedience to God's Will, made all respect him to a degree that was almost veneration. He had, however, to bear the most violent and cruel treatment from his brother, whose part was invariably taken by their tutor, who accompanied them to Vienna. The tutor, a Lutheran, also tried to persuade Stanislaus to moderate his devotions and practices of mortification, and conform more to the customs of the world, telling him that all such things were superfluous, and that he could be sure of his soul's salvation without them. But the youth was proof no less against the worldly prudence of his tutor than the cruelties of his brother, who often gave him angry words and even blows.

For two years, the saint suffered these harassing persecutions without a word of anger or of complaint, and found that his devotion was increased, rather than diminished, by them. Soon after he was sixteen he became seriously ill, and, when he recovered he made application to the Provincial for Southern Germany to be admitted into the Society of Jesus by blessed Peter Canisius who was then in Rome.

In the summer following his entrance into the Novitiate, when his life seemed to have become a constant prayer, his body grew progressively weaker. He passed away from a world which had no attraction for him, early in the morning of 15th August, 1568, the feast of the Assumption, while he was still only eighteen.

Bl. Ralph Sherwine

Died 1581

MY dearest Uncle,

      After many conflicts, mixed with spiritual consolations and Christian comforts, it hath pleased God, of His infinite mercy, to call me out of this vale of misery. To Him, therefore, for all His benefits, all times and for ever be all praise and glory.

    Your tender care always had over me, and cost bestowed on me, I trust in heaven shall be rewarded. My prayers you have still had, and that was but duty; other tokens of a grateful mind I could not show by reason of my restrained necessity.

    This very morning, which is the festival of *St. Andrew*, I was advertised by superior authority that tomorrow I was to end the course of this life. God grant that I may do it to the imitation of this noble apostle and servant of God, and that with Joy I may say, rising off the hurdle, *Salve sancta crux, etc.*

    Innocency is my only comfort against all the forged villainy which is fathered on my fellow priests and me. Well, when by the High Judge, God Himself, this false vizard of treason shall be removed from true Catholic men's faces, then shall it appear who they be that carry a well-meaning, and who an evil, murdering mind. In the mean season, God forgive all injustice, and if it be His blessed will to convert our persecutors, that they may become professors of His truth.

    Prayers for my soul procure for me, my loving patron:

and so, having great need to prepare myself for God, never quieter in mind, nor less troubled towards God, binding all my iniquities up in His precious wounds, I bid you farewell; yea, and once again, the lovingest uncle that ever kinsman had in this world, farewell.

God grant us both His grace and blessing until the end, that, living in His fear and dying in His favour, we may enjoy one the other for ever. Salute all my fellow Catholics. And so, without further troubling of you, my sweetest benefactor, farewell. On *St. Andrew's Day,* 1581.

Your cousin,

RALPH SHERWINE, *Priest*

RALPH SHERWINE was a native of Derbyshire, and became a Fellow of Exeter College, Oxford, where he was considered an excellent philosopher and Greek and Hebrew scholar. In the year 1575 he abandoned his position and prospects under the Church of England and went to Douai College to be received into the Catholic Church. In due time he was ordained priest, and then journeyed to Rome to pursue his studies. He was to have accompanied Dr. Goldwell, the Bishop of St. Asaph, who was going to England to confirm some Catholics; but the Bishop was taken ill at Rheims, and Sherwine had to pursue his journey alone. In London he began his mission with alacrity, but was soon arrested in the house of a Catholic, and thrown into the Marshalsea prison.

A proposal for a disputation on religion was offered to him and other priests who were there, which was eagerly accepted; but before it could take place he was called up for repeated examinations and torture on the rack. After this, offers of the highest preferment were made to him, if he would consent to go to St. Paul's church. His preparation for death was most devout and when the hangman came to lay hands on him, he reverently kissed the blood of his fellow-martyr, Edmund Campion, with which the man's hands were stained.

St. *Joseph Calasanctius*

1556–1628

BE of good heart, and rest assured the institute will stand. Do not believe that our Order, though it seems to be so, is destroyed (through what means God knows) as it should never rise again; nevertheless, by the assistance of our Lord, it will become more ample than ever, and I think before very long, too. Be constant, and you shall see the half of God over you: that you yield not to sorrow, but that your virtue may appear more bright in tribulation. As long as I live, I will hope against life; because the work which I did, was done merely for the love of God.

JOSEPH CALASANCTIUS was born of a noble family at Petralta in Aragon on 15th September, 1556. Having heard, when he was only five years old, that the Devil was the enemy of God, he ran through every nook of his father's mansion in search of this terrible being, whom in his simplicity he thought he could destroy. Nor did this desire to slay the enemy of souls leave the little Joseph after the first search for him. One day, he quietly slipped out into the street and begged all the children he saw to go with him to seek the Devil, that he might drive him quite out of the world. From his tender years he began to show that fondness for children, and that gift of instructing them, for which he was afterwards so distinguished. He called them around him when he was still but a child himself, and taught them the Catholic Faith and godly prayers.

When he grew up, his father wished him to maintain the military glories of the family; his own desire was to be a soldier of the Cross. Eventually he became a priest in consequence of a vow, which his father permitted him to make, when his recovery from a dangerous illness seemed almost impossible. He was soon invited by many bishops in the kingdoms of New Castile, Aragon, and Catalonia to help them in their work, wherein he surpassed the hopes of all in restoring Church discipline, and marvellously putting an end to hatreds and feuds. But an inward voice, which he found irresistible, summoned him to Rome. When he reached the Holy City, his heart was moved by the vice and ignorance of the children of the poor, and as a result he founded the Congregation of Pious Schools. He himself provided all that was necessary for the education of the children, receiving nothing from them in payment; and there were soon above a thousand children of every rank under his care. For fifty-two years St. Joseph underwent so many toils and patiently bore so many griefs that he was acclaimed by all men. Soon he began to feel the pressure of debt and anxiety in maintaining such vast numbers of children and poor depending upon him for subsistance. Yet he had harder trials to come. Calumny, scorn, injustice, were allowed to try the saint. He was arrested upon a charge of which he was both ignorant and innocent; and, at the age of eighty-six, was led through the streets to prison.

Within the space of a year he was proved innocent. But the trials of the saint were not ended; others attempted to malign him, yet his resignation remained as perfect as it had ever been.

On Christmas Eve, 1598, the Tiber overflowed its banks so alarmingly as to occasion a terrible inundation in and around Rome; the waters covered a considerable part of the city, forcing their way through doors and windows, and destroying both life and property to a terrible extent. The courageous efforts of Joseph on this occasion have never been forgotten. He plunged into the waters and waded through them regardless of danger or fatigue; and, as he was very tall of stature, he was able to save many from drowning, and to drag out many dead bodies for Christian burial; sometimes it was his object to open a passage, and give vent to the stagnant water; at other times, he procured a boat, and allowing himself no respite, went backwards and forwards to convey provisions to the needy, rescuing those who were the least secure, though at his own great risk; everywhere was he to be seen at work, apparently unwearied and unweariable.

At last the illness which was to close his life began. His fortitude and patience were indeed marvellous, for his powers were great. However, on the 25th day of August, 1648, being ninety-two years of age, he calmly expired with the thrice-uttered name of Jesus upon his lips.

Bl. Jane Lestonnac

1556–1640

MY dear good Sister, I was just longing to hear from you when Sister Madeleine sent me the news that you were more than usually ill. I am so disturbed that, even with all my own infirmities, I am going to ask to have them increased by half of yours, in order to relieve you. The share our Lord gives you of His cross shows me how much He loves you, since He does not wish to relieve you of it. Let us encourage ourselves to bear it constantly, since He is pleased to call us after Him.

*

MY dear daughter, the harvest is great and extensive, and the labourers are few, as Our Saviour said. Since He is the master of the harvest, I have asked Him to send you to work there as faithful labourers. With the help of His goodness and your virtue I hope it will be a success. He has not thought me worthy of serving Him in this undertaking. This honour and glory He has reserved for you. I hope through His mercy that what I have sown in tears, you will reap in joy, and that Toulouse will not be for you what it was for me—a sterile land abounding in contradiction— but that you will find it fruitful in grace. However, should it please divine Providence to ordain otherwise, you must accept with resignation, whatever treatment may be meted out to you. It will be just and will make you like your Mother. It will also help you to realize that we are all useless servants where the advancement of God's glory is concerned and that we must write the success of our labours as well as our reward for the Goodness.

★

WITH regard to my health my age [almost eighty] can only mean infirmities for me, for by God's grace, I have these in plenty to make me practise patience. If I get one good day in the week, the rest are a torture. A slow fever is slowly but surely sapping my strength, and this makes me strive constantly to become worthy of going to God. I think of nothing else.

BL. JANE LESTONNAC, or de l'Estonnac, Marquise de Montferrant-Landiras, was born on 2nd February, 1556. She was founder of the Order of Daughters of Notre Dame. Her father was a counsellor in the parliament of Bordeaux, and came of the ancient and distinguished family of Lestonnac. Her mother, Jeanne Deyquem de Montaigne, was sister of the famous philosopher.

At seventeen she married Gaston, Marquis de Montferrant-Landiras, one of the most illustrious families of Guienne. She had been a happy wife for more than twenty-four years when the Marquis died. Jeanne resolved to retire from the world, but waited until her four surviving children were settled in life. One of her daughters married the Baron d'Arpaillant; two others became nuns. In 1603 Jeanne entered the convent of the Feuillantines at Toulouse. She had been there only six months when the unaccustomed austerities of the cloister affected her health so seriously that she had to give up the idea of becoming a nun there, and she returned to her relations at Bordeaux. While she was overwhelmed with disappointment at the failure of her plan, she conceived the idea of founding a new Order for educational purposes. She spent some time in prayerful seclusion, near her son's château at Landiras, and then she founded the institute of Daughters of our Lady, which was annexed to the Order of St. Benedict. The new Order was established by a decree of Paul V in 1607. Jeanne and her first few disciples took the veil in the following year, in their house near the port in Bordeaux. Many convents of the Order have been established since then and have taken an active part in the education of the young. She died on 2nd February, 1640, at the age of eighty-four. She was at once regarded as a saint, and articles which had belonged to her were preserved as inestimable treasures. Her canonization was talked of from the time of her death, but it was only in September, 1900, that she was solemnly beatified by Leo XIII.

The second letter is dated 1631, and the third 26th June, 1635.

Bl. Robert Southwell

1561–1595

UNDERSTANDING that you were resolved upon a course which most nearly toucheth the salvation of your soul, I received such contentment as a sincere and most faithful love feeleth in the long desired happiness of so dear a friend. But hearing since, that you will dwell in danger and linger in new delays, my hopes hang in suspense, and my heart in grief, angry with the chains that thus enthral you, and sorry to see you captive to your own fears. Shrine not any longer a dead soul in a living body; bail reason out of senses' prison, that after so long a bondage in sin, you may enjoy your former liberty in God's Church, and free your thought from the servile awe of uncertain perils. If all should take effect, that your timorous surmises suggest, yet could not even the misery of your present state, with the loss of your patronage, and keeping you in this disfavour of God, have either left you any greater benefit to lose, or any deeper infelicity to incur. Weigh with yourself at how easy a price you rate God, Whom you are content to sell for the use of your substance, yea, and for the preventing a loss which haply will never ensue. Have you so little need of Him, that you can so long forbear Him? or is He so worthless in your estimation that you will venture nothing for Him? Adjourn not, I pray you, a matter of such importance. Remember that one sin begetteth another, and when you yield to nurse daily this venomous brood in your breast, what can you look for, but, that like vipers, they should compass your destruction.

Custom soon groweth to a second nature, and being once master of the mind, it can hardly be cast out of possession. If today you find yourself faint, fainter you are like to be tomorrow, if you languish in the same distaste without cure, and suffer the corrosive of sin to consume you without opposing its violence. How can you flatter yourself with an ungrounded hope of mercy, since to continue in it so long, is the surest way to stop the fountain of it for ever? The more you offend God, the less you deserve His favour; and to be deaf when He calleth you, is to close His ears against all cries in the time of your necessity. If you mean to surrender your heart to Him, why do you lend so much leisure to the devil to strengthen his hold: and why stop up the passages with mire by which the pure waters of grace must flow into your soul? Look if you can upon a crucifix without blushing; do but count the five wounds of Christ once over without a bleeding conscience. Read your sins in those characters, and examine your thoughts whether the sight do please them. Alas! if that innocent blood move you not, or if you can find still in your heart to open afresh such undeserved wounds, I would I might send you the sacrifice of my dearest veins, to try whether nature could awake remorse, and prepare a way for grace's entrance. Sorrow puts me to silence, and therefore, Brother, I must end, desiring you to have pity on yourself, whose harms make so bitter an impression on Ager's mind. God of His infinite goodness strengthen you in all your good designments.

THIS great English poet was born at Horsham St. Faith's in Norfolk in 1561 and became a Jesuit at Rome at the age of seventeen; he came on the English mission in 1586. Southwell was a poet and prose-writer (best known for *The Burning Babe* and *Triumphs Over Death*), who in all probability had an effect on the work of Shakespeare himself. He was betrayed to the State in 1592 and imprisoned for three years before he was brought to trial, being tortured thirteen times by the notorious Richard Topcliffe, and was finally hanged, drawn and quartered, to the indignation of many in the crowd of onlookers. In a special sense he was a martyr for the sacrament of Penance, for he was trapped by a girl who pretended to want confession and then warned the police. He was beatified in 1929.

The above letter was written to his brother.

BIBLIOGRAPHY

BESIDES the numerous official documents concerning the various individual saints, the following brief list of collated lives will be of service.

The Encyclopædia Britannica

The Catholic Encyclopædia

Heroic Virtue, by Pope Benedict XIV

Breviarium Romanum

The Dictionary of National Biography

Great Catholics (Ed. Claude Williamson)

Great Spiritual Writers, by Claude Williamson

Manual of Patrology, by F. Cayré

Lives of the Saints, by Alban Butler (Ed. Thurston and Attwater)

The Saints in Christian Art, by Mrs. A. Bell

The Missionary Priests, by Bishop Challoner

Church Dedications, by E. Arnold Foster

Dictionary of Christian Biography, by Smith and Wace

The Faces of the Saints, by W. Schamoni

Patrology, by Otto Bardenhewer

Lives of the English Martyrs (Ed. Dom Bede Camm)

Dictionary of Saintly Women, by A. B. C. Dunbar

Sacred and Legendary Art, by Mrs. Jameson

Miniature Lives, by H. S. Bowen.

The Saints of Italy, by Lucy Menzies

A Biographical Dictionary of Saints, by F. G. Holweck

The Book of Saints (A. and C. Black)

Menology of England and Wales, by R. Stanton

Supplementary volume to Butler's *Lives of the Fathers, Martyrs and other Saints,* by Bernard Kelly

Daily Lections (Ed. J. F. W. Bullock)

Lives of the Saints, by S. Baring-Gould

The Liturgical Year, by Dom Prosper Guéranger

Lives of the Saints (Ed. Newman)

Saints are not Sad (Ed. F. Sheed)

Emblems of Saints, by F. C. Husenbeth

Canonization and Authority, by E. W. Kemp

Saints and their Attributes, by G. Helen Roeder

Library of the Fathers (Ed. Pusey, Keble and Newman)

Ante-Nicene Christian Library (Ed. Roberts and Donaldson)

Enchiridion Symbolarum et Definitionum, by H. Denzinger